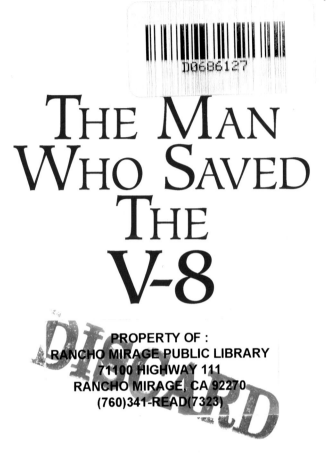

THE MAN WHO SAVED THE V-8

THE MAN WHO SAVED THE V-8

*The Untold Stories
of Some of the
Most Important Product Decisions
in the History of
Ford Motor Company*

By Chase Morsey Jr.

*To my wife Beverly, who at the age of ninety-six,
continues to inspire me everyday.*

Table of Contents

Introduction

In the spring of 1949, I stood in the boardroom of the Ford Motor Company, across the table from Henry Ford II, Ernest Breech, Robert McNamara, and the other leaders of what was then one of the most powerful companies in the world.

These men were titans of American industry. Ford was the grandson of Henry Ford himself. His name was on the side of the building—and on about a third of all the cars and trucks on the road. Breech was the executive he had hired away from General Motors to transform his struggling company into a modern corporation. McNamara was one of the legendary "Whiz Kids" then in the process of taking Ford even further.

I was a twenty-nine-year-old product analyst who had been hired just a few months before. I did not know much about running a car company, but I did know one thing for certain: these men had made one of the worst decisions in the history of the Ford Motor Company. They had decided to kill the Ford V-8. And I was determined to talk them out of it.

Ford introduced its famous flathead V-8 in 1932. At the time, such big engines were only found in the most expensive luxury automobiles. They powered Cadillacs and Lincolns and left more pedestrian powertrains in the dust. But Henry Ford had decided the common man deserved that kind of power too, and he was determined to give it to him.

At the time, Ford was lagging behind its archrival, Chevrolet. The company that had put the world on wheels seemed unable to keep up with General Motors' upstart brand. But the V-8 would change all of that. The powerful motor would allow Ford to catch up with Chevy and pass it to reclaim the title of best-selling brand in America.

The Ford V-8 would become the car of choice for everyone who loved speed. Police quickly adopted them as pursuit vehicles. So did the criminals they were pursuing. John Dillinger and Clyde Barrow both sent laudatory notes to Henry Ford, thanking him for producing such a fine automobile. The engine made Ford's name in the world of motorsports—and made that name an acronym that stood for "First On Race Day." The V-8 was why legions of loyal customers stuck with the brand, even when it lagged in other areas.

I knew that, because I was one of them.

My first car was a Ford V-8, and I had owned them ever since. I had driven my Fords back and forth across the country, reveling in their speed and the nods of admiration they garnered from other driving enthusiasts. Whenever I stopped to fill up my gas tank, the men who manned the pumps would linger under the hood, listening to the rumble of that big engine. Mechanics would wander out to discuss its many merits. Other drivers would smile and give me a thumbs-up.

Despite the success of the V-8, Ford had struggled during the 1940s because of rampant mismanagement. By the time I joined the company, Breech and his team were trying to dig their way out from underneath mounting losses. They were General Motors men who had Chevrolet in their blood, and Chevy still did not have a V-8. And since Chevrolet was, again, outselling Ford, Breech and his boys reckoned Ford did not need one either. It was just an added expense that made the company's cars more expensive and less competitive. But the V-8 was also the heart and soul of the Ford Motor Company. It was what was made a Ford a Ford. Killing the vaunted V-8 would kill Ford. I knew it, and I was prepared to prove it.

I had spent the past three months preparing my case as carefully as any trial lawyer. I had sent researchers out across the country to talk to customers and dealers and owners of competing products. This was some of the most detailed market research ever conducted by a corporation, and it provided me with the data I needed to prove my point.

I had also worked with Ford's manufacturing experts to figure out a way to produce the V-8 more efficiently and, therefore, less expensively. As a young officer in the U.S. Army Air Forces' Statistical Control Group, I had learned the power of numbers. I had used them to help America wage war against enemies in Europe and Asia. And I was now ready to employ them in a more personal fight to save one of the greatest engines ever—and the company that made it.

To this day, I have no idea how a young, newly hired manager like myself, who was still on probation and had yet to eat in the executive dining room or see my name inscribed on the bonus rolls, had the nerve to challenge the most powerful men inside the Ford Motor Company and tell them they were wrong.

But that is exactly what I did.

As a result, Ford reversed its decision to kill the V-8. It would prove a potent engine for Ford's prosperity in those golden years of American automotive supremacy. It would go on to power some of the most iconic automobiles ever made. Cars like the Ford Thunderbird and Mustang.

I had a hand in those as well. Over the next thirteen years, I would play a central role in some of the most pivotal decisions in Ford's history—decisions that changed the course of the company and helped establish many of the practices that are now considered central to the success of any automaker. I worked side by side with men like Lewis Crusoe and Lee Iacocca. I also contended with federal grand juries and notorious mobsters. And I learned many important lessons—lessons that have proved invaluable to me throughout my business career.

This is my story.

Chapter One

MY LOVE AFFAIR
WITH FORDS

It is not my intention to write an autobiography. However, I do think it is important to know a few things about my background in order to understand how these formative experiences gave me the insight and ability to make important decisions during my career at the Ford Motor Company.

I have always loved to drive. Ever since I was a small boy, I have been fascinated with automobiles and felt the tug of the open road. I would ride my bicycle all over town, and would stop along the busiest roads and just sit there, watching the cars go by. From the start, the ones that caught my eye were the Fords.

I was born in St. Louis, Missouri, on December 11, 1919. I did not inherit any family business or wealth; all my parents gave me was a great education, the desire to succeed, and the skills to be successful—my parents gave me those things and their deep and unselfish love that has been a lifelong source of inspiration and strength.

My father, Chase Morsey, was a lawyer, just like his father and his father before him. I assumed I would become a lawyer, too. He was a quiet man but very intelligent. He also was an avid golfer and introduced me to the game when I was old enough to swing a club.

My mother was born Ruth Callicutt. She came from a small hamlet in Illinois but had been to college—still a rare thing for a woman in those days. She was more outgoing than my father. I was more like her, open and talkative. My mother was the leading influence in my life. She instilled in me the will and desire to succeed, and she made sure I had the skills necessary to do so. It was my mother, not my father, who taught me to drive. My father never would have had the patience.

Those lessons took place in the family Buick. To my mother, driving was one more skill that would be important for me to possess as I made my way into the wide world. She was determined to teach me, even if it meant enduring the excruciating sound of grinding gears. She and I would drive out to Forest Park, that sea of green in the heart of St. Louis that had been home to the 1904 World's Fair and the Summer Olympics. It was close to our apartment, and a maze of gently curving roads ran through the park, making it the perfect place for a novice motorist to learn how to handle an automobile. Mother would wince as I struggled to find the right gear. It took me a long time to master the clutch, but she never lost her patience. There were no automatics in those days, so she knew I had to figure it out. We spent hours out there in the Buick, until I finally did.

I got my license when I turned sixteen. By then, my parents had enrolled me in the prestigious Country Day School. I participated in as many school activities as I could. One of them was selling ads for the student newspaper and yearbook, and I sometimes borrowed the Buick when father was not using it so that I could call on local merchants after class.

One day, during my junior year, I came home from school and saw a new Ford Coupe sitting in the driveway. It was dark blue, with white sidewall tires, and it looked gorgeous! My mother had persuaded my father that I was old enough to have a car of my own.

The Ford was a complete surprise to me. I had no idea that my parents were planning to buy me a car of my own—let alone a new V-8. That car was the living end to me. I just loved that automobile, and I loved driving it! I drove that Ford so much I wore out the first set of tires in just three months. My father was really upset by that, but it showed how much I loved being behind the wheel. In those first three months, I put over 10,000 miles on the odometer—and I never even left town. That is how much I loved to drive.[1]

I spent the summer after graduation from Country Day traveling across the country. A classmate of mine had a sister in California, and an invitation from her was all the persuading we needed to hit the road. We drove through almost every state west of the Mississippi and saw many of the great national parks: the Grand Canyon, Crater Lake, Bryce Canyon, and Zion. The trip lasted six weeks. I returned just in time to pack my bags and board the eastbound train for Amherst, Massachusetts.

>—<>—<

Thinking back, there was never much discussion about me going to school anywhere but Amherst College. My Sunday-school teacher was an Amherst graduate. So was the assistant headmaster at Country Day. One of my father's close friends had gone to Amherst as well. In those days, St. Louis had a strong Amherst alumni community. In fact, during my first year at Amherst there were thirty-three boys from St. Louis at the college—more than from any other city in the country. I knew nothing about the school. I had never visited the campus before applying for admission. I was simply told that was where I was going. So I packed, said good-bye to my parents, and got on the train to Massachusetts, with four of my classmates from Country Day.

I did well academically, joined the Delta Kappa Epsilon fraternity, and also found an opportunity to hone my business skills. I won a spot on the school newspaper, the *Amherst Student*, selling advertising. It was a coveted position, and I beat out many other students to get it. But with

---

1 That love of driving would stay with me all my life. Later, when I moved to California, I would drive to Texas and back each year to check on my oil business. I could have flown, but I preferred being behind the wheel. I have driven all the way across the United States and back again twice. When I was in my eighties, my wife and I drove all the way from California to Alaska. It was an 8,000-mile trip, but I had wanted to drive the Alcan Highway all my life and never had. Our friends all thought we were crazy, but we had a great time. I am in my nineties now, but I still drive almost every day.

my experience from Country Day, I excelled at it. However, I missed having a car to make my sales calls.

I still had my Ford Coupe when I left for college. By then, I had tricked it out with a spotlight and other accessories. Unfortunately, we were not allowed to have a car at Amherst during our freshman year, so I had to leave it back home in St. Louis. But by the time spring break rolled around, I had come up with a plan. I took the train home, drove my Ford back to school, and went to see Dean Porter.

"Sir, I have a car, and it's in the public garage in downtown Amherst. Here are the keys," I said, handing them across his desk before he could object. "I want it because I'm selling advertising for the *Amherst Student*. You keep these keys. I'm not going to be going out at night or sneaking back and forth to Smith College. I just want it for work."

He smiled and agreed.

In the afternoons, if I did not have any classes, I would go up and see the dean's secretary and get the keys. We became really close friends. I would go around town selling ads then come back and return the keys. I never had one problem with Dean Porter, and he never had one problem with me. He used to kid me and say, "You still got that car?" And I'd say, "Yes, sir, I have!"

From that spring on, I would drive my Ford back and forth between Amherst and St. Louis a couple of times each year.[2] I stopped at a lot of gas stations along the way, and I spent a lot of time talking to folks about my car and its powerful V-8 motor. There was no self-service in those days—it was strictly full-service. Each time I pulled into a new service station, the attendant would come out, fill the tank, wash the windshield, and then pop the hood and whistle.

"I see you got one of those Ford V-8s," they would say.

"Yep!" I would reply proudly.

"Is she fast?"

"She sure is!"

---

2 In the wintertime, I would take the train home for the holidays, as the roads would become too treacherous in the snow.

Other motorists noticed my car, too. "You got a V-8 in there?" they would ask me.

"Yep," I would say with a smile.

"Wow! You've got the best!"

Owning a V-8 Ford was a real point of pride for me, because I could see how impressed people who knew about cars were with mine. I would usually stop at the same service stations on each trip, so I got to know some of those attendants pretty well. And they never stopped asking me about my Ford V-8.

During my sophomore year, I became circulation manager for the *Amherst Student*. I came up with the idea of writing a letter to all of the parents, offering them a subscription to the newspaper so that they could keep track of what their sons were up to at school. It was a huge success. The subscription forms came flooding in, and I was promoted to business manager. It was one of the biggest honors of my college career, and I made enough money working on the newspaper to go down to the local Ford dealer in Springfield and trade in my Coupe for a new Ford sedan. It was maroon, with white sidewall tires and, of course, a V-8 under the hood. My father was sure impressed the next time I came home and pulled into the driveway. He could not believe that I had been able to buy a new car on my own, without any help from him or anyone else while I was still in college.

The service-station attendants were just as impressed with my new Ford as they had been with my old Coupe. And they kept commenting on its potent V-8. I put a lot of miles on those cars, driving between Massachusetts and Missouri, but I never got into an accident in either one of them. I was always a very careful driver, and those cars were my pride and joy.

⋙⋘

I maintained pretty good grades all the way through my four years at Amherst and graduated *cum laude*, with honors, in history. I assumed I would be going to law school next. I had never wanted to be anything but a lawyer. I had grown up listening to my father argue about cases with his friends and colleagues. I knew how respected he was in the community and how famous my grandfather had been before him. I wanted to follow in their footsteps.

As my time at Amherst drew to an end, the dean took me aside and assured me that I would be able to get into whatever law school I chose. "You've got grades that are good enough to get into either Yale or Harvard. It should be easy for you," he said. "You're going to be graduating with honors, and Amherst is well thought of by both schools."

So, as I made the long drive back to St. Louis for spring break in 1941, all I was thinking about was preparing my applications. But when I arrived home, I found my father in a somber mood. He asked me to come into the living room so that we could have a talk, and he got right to the point.

"Look, son, I know you want to be lawyer, and I'm very happy about that. But this country is going to get into a war soon. You're going to get partway through law school, and you're going to get drafted, and you're going to have absolutely nothing to offer the army—no skills at all. You'll be nothing but cannon fodder," Father said as he handed me a magazine. "I've bought some stock in a little company called IBM. There's an article here in *Fortune* about them. I want you to read it. You'll notice that they have a sales school located in Endicott, which is not far from Route 20. You pass right by there when you drive through New York. I want you to go down there and talk to the guy. Find out what they can offer you and what you can offer them."

That conversation changed my whole life.

The article was very impressive. It talked about Tom Watson and the company he was building—a company that was already changing the way businesses were run. IBM sold typewriters and time clocks, but its most exciting and profitable products were tabulating machines. These were the forerunners of the computer. Though primitive by today's standards, they were the cutting edge of technology in the early 1940s, and one company after another was adopting them to automate an array of business processes. Though I had never entertained the idea of working for a large corporation, it seemed like exciting stuff. So I took my father's advice and left a day early so that I would have time to stop in Endicott on my way back to Amherst.

I was amazed when I arrived. Endicott was an old mill town, but Watson had transformed it into a modern corporate enclave. In addition to IBM's factories, there were research-and-development labs, as well as offices and a company school. Watson had even built a country club for his employees that they could join for just five dollars a month.

He was the most farsighted executive I have ever known. He paid his workers far more than the standard union wage, making it impossible for any of the labor syndicates to gain a foothold in his factories. Salaried employees were also well taken care of. He was way ahead of his time when it came to how to treat employees and maintain a high level of morale and productivity.

I checked into the local hotel and called the sales school. I soon had an appointment with the director, Charlie Love.

"What are you doing here?" Love asked me after I was ushered into his office.

I told him the truth. I told him about how I had wanted to be a lawyer but had been urged by my father to learn a skill that would keep me from being mere cannon fodder in the war he believed was imminent. I told him about the *Fortune* article and how impressed I was to read about Mr. Watson and IBM.

Love smiled. "I've got twenty-five of my branch managers out interviewing seniors, and you're up here interviewing me," he chuckled. "You're hired!"

After I graduated from Amherst a few months later, I was back in Endicott, surrounded by rooms filled with arcane machinery and webs of wiring, struggling to make sense of it all. It was July of 1941. There were seventy-seven students in Sales School Number 525, both men and women. The men were being trained as salesmen; the women as assistant engineers. Once they graduated, they would go out into the field and help set up the machines and train the operators at the companies that leased our equipment.

The men were put up at the hotel. There were two of us to a room, and we took our meals there as well. The women lived in a building of their own, out at the country club. I was one of the only guys with a car, so I had a lot of friends. I joined the country club and played golf out there on weekends.

The sales school lasted nearly five months. The faculty was made up of IBM employees, who taught us about the technical details of the machines and how to use them. Before we could sell them, we had to learn how they worked and what they could do. It turned out they could do quite a lot—everything from payroll and inventory management to sales analysis and cost accounting. A keypunch operator entered all of the data into a machine that spit out punch cards that were then sorted and fed into a tabulating machine that crunched the numbers and generated reports. It was complicated stuff—you had to have some brains just figure the damn things out—and none of us knew anything about them before we started. But I knew how to sell things, and I was confident I could sell these machines.

Once my training was finished, it was assumed that I would return to St. Louis and work at the IBM office there. However, I was eager to prove myself, and I knew that it would be too easy to do well in a city where everyone knew my father and respected him. I went to see Love and asked him to put me somewhere else where I could make my mark relying only on my own skills and abilities.

"Mr. Love, look, in St. Louis everyone knows my father," I told him. "I want to find out if I can do this on my own. I want to find out if I'm really any good at it."

"Fine," he said. "I'll send you to New Haven."

That was how, on November 1, 1941, I found myself in Connecticut, in a small office on Whitney Avenue, not far from Yale University. I did not know anything about the city. That suited me perfectly, as I would have to rely solely on my own talents. The branch manager was George Patterson. He was a good mentor. He gave me a desk and told me to work with the other salesman until I learned the ropes.

I found that my experience selling for the newspapers at Amherst and Country Day really came in handy. I had developed a real ability to talk to people. I was not afraid to walk in the door of new business, say hello, and ask to talk to someone in charge. I enjoyed the work. It became something of a game for me. We weren't just selling toothpaste or wrenches; we were selling a new way of doing things. I regarded each client as a new puzzle. I had to analyze their business operations and figure out where IBM machines could be used to improve them. I didn't yet realize that if it didn't work out, you didn't get paid. I just assumed it would work out.

The biggest challenge for me was understanding the equipment and how to make it work—the technical side of wiring the boards and running the cards through the machine. I had to create a system for the customer, and each one was different. There were unique exceptions to the rules at every company. It wasn't always one and one make two; sometimes it was one plus three minus two makes two. You had to be flexible. That was the hard part. Selling the machines was easy, at least for me.

IBM already had a great reputation in business circles. Most of the companies I called on were already using our typewriters or time clocks, and most of them had heard about the tabulating machines but were not sure how the machines could help them. My secret was taking prospective clients to our customers' businesses so that they could see how our customers were using our machines. I made those existing customers my assistant salesmen. Most of them were so proud of their IBM machines that they were happy to oblige. They were so much more persuasive than I ever could have been. They were the best sales tools I had.

When I started at the company in 1941, IBM manufactured the tabulating machines and leased them to its customers. A small company might bring in income of five or six hundred a month, while larger companies could generate as much as $10,000 a month. As a salesman, I received a base salary, plus commission. I looked in the newspaper and found a room for rent. It was a pretty modest beginning, but I was having fun. I still had my maroon Ford, and I put a lot of miles on it calling on customers.

During my free time, I liked to go to the movies. That's where I was on Sunday, December 7, 1941. The lights came on in the middle of the picture, and the film was stopped. The manager came out in front of the screen and shouted, "The Japanese just bombed Pearl Harbor!"

Here we go, I thought. I was glad that I had listened to my father.

I received my draft notice in September 1942. The army was kind enough to give me the option of reporting for induction either in Connecticut or back home in Missouri. I chose the latter so that I could say good-bye to my parents before heading off to my uncertain future. It was an emotional visit, and it was soon over.

On October 15, I boarded a bus and headed for the Jefferson Barracks, an old army base south of St. Louis. It did not have a good reputation, and I discovered that was entirely warranted. There were fifty of us in each room, and I could not sleep because of all the snoring. We all shared the same bath facilities, too, and had to stand in line for everything—showers, sinks, and toilets. But the worst lines were at the mess hall. Sometimes I had to wait forever to get my meals, and the food we received only added insult to injury.

I was in pretty good shape when I entered the service, so basic training was not that difficult for me. But waiting in all those lines was torture. Fortunately, I was only there for a short time before receiving orders to report to Knollwood Field in North Carolina.

"What's this all about?" I asked the second lieutenant in charge of our group of recruits.

"I'm not sure," he said. "But I think that's where they're training guys to go over to Africa."

Operation Torch, the Anglo-American invasion of North Africa, had just begun. Our green troops were slogging it out with Rommel's *Afrika Korps* veterans and paying dearly for every mile they liberated. When I told my mother I would be training to go to Africa, she burst into tears. The day I left for North Carolina, our train stopped at Union Station in St. Louis. We were not allowed into the civilian area, but I could see my mother standing at the gate, waving. I ran up to her and grabbed her hand through the bars.

"Don't worry," I told her. "I'll be OK."

I hoped that was true.

I got off the train in Southern Pines, North Carolina. A sergeant met me at the station, escorted me to an automobile, and drove me to the Mid Pines Inn, a luxurious resort near Pinehurst. I soon found myself in a nice, private room with a sunken bath. I took my meals in the main dining room, which served delicious fare, and did not even have to stand in line to eat. And there were beautiful golf courses all around me. Pinehurst itself was right down the road. So I called home and asked my parents to send me my clubs.

Maybe the army won't be so bad after all, I thought, even as I waited for the other shoe to drop.

It never did. A short walk through the woods led to the Pine Needles Lodge, which had been turned into the headquarters of the U.S. Army Air Forces' Technical Training Command.[3] There was a nice hotel, a beautiful golf course, and a long, low-rise building below that housed an IBM installation. As soon as I saw the IBM machines, I knew I wasn't going to North Africa, and I breathed easy. But it turned out that they were in real trouble.

The guys there were supposed to prepare a regular personnel report for the commanding general, Walter Weaver, who was in charge of the Army Air Forces' Technical Training Command. They were in the process of trying to automate these reports, but they

---

3 The army commandeered the property in April 1942.

just couldn't seem to get it right. The captain in charge asked if I could help. These reports had formerly been prepared manually and required fifteen clerks five days to complete. I designed a new system that allowed the whole task to be completed by one IBM operator in twelve hours. After the first one was run, the senior officers compared it to the manual report. They found a dozen errors—all of them in the manual report.

One day, as I was working on one of the machines, General Weaver himself came into the room and asked the captain if there was someone who could caddy for him. The captain called me over.

"Private Morsey likes to play golf," he said. "And he's the one who fixed your personnel report."

As he teed up on the first hole, the general started asking me about my background. I told him about Amherst and IBM as we walked in between shots. The first hole was wide open, in plain view of the lodge, but the next sixteen were back in the woods. When we got to the second tee, he looked around to see if there was anyone else in sight. There was no one. He asked me to join him. I used his clubs and played the next sixteen holes with the general. As we approached the eighteenth tee, I took his bag and resumed caddying. On the way back to the clubhouse, General Weaver said he was quite impressed with how I had sorted out the mess with his personnel reports.

"There's no use in you staying here, caddying for me," he said. "I'm sending you to OCS."

After a few weeks at Officer Candidate School in Miami Beach, Florida, I was told to report to a nearby hotel. There I was escorted to a room where an officer was conducting interviews. He introduced himself as James Wright, and he proceeded to ask me about my experience at IBM and my knowledge of their machines.

"I'm interviewing men for a new branch of the Air Forces[4] called Statistical Control," he told me. "If selected, you will complete your OCS

4 What would become the U.S. Air Force was then a branch of the army, known as the Army Air Forces. It became a separate branch of the military in 1947.

training at Harvard Business School. After that, you will be assigned to an IBM installation."

I had no idea what statistical control meant. He just as well might have told me that he was setting up a gin joint. But the word Harvard sure got my attention. I must have done OK in the interview, because instead of being sent to North Africa, I was ordered to report to Cambridge, Massachusetts, to one of the top business schools in the country.

⤜⬥⬥⤛

One of my teachers at Harvard was Robert McNamara. He was a tall, thin guy, with glasses, who was smart as hell. He was one of the brightest people I had ever met. He was the youngest professor the university's business school ever had, and he had been assigned to teach us about analytical methods that had been developed for business, but which the Army Air Forces believed might have applications in the air war against Germany and Japan.[5] I thought he was great. Although he was icy and could be somewhat severe, he obviously knew more than any of us about the subjects he was teaching.

Our wartime task quickly became clear: We would collect data about every single aircraft in the Army Air Forces—about every mission they flew and about the results of those sorties on our enemies. We would use that data to keep the planes in the air, to allocate men and resources, and to fine-tune tactics and strategy to maximize the impact our pilots and bomber crews were having on the Axis war effort. It would be a whole new way of waging war. We had to learn how to fight, not with bullets and bombs, but with numbers. In its January 23, 1943, edition, *Time* magazine described it as, "a new kind of field duty that is a cross between war and big business," that was designed to boost the Army Air Forces' "profits."

---

5 McNamara was commissioned as a captain in the Army Air Forces while we were studying under him at Harvard.

"By instituting a management-control system, General Arnold hopes to up those profits in terms of damage to the enemy and conservation of U.S. men and equipment," the magazine wrote.

To do that, we had to not only master this new field of statistical analysis but also learn about the different aircraft in our arsenal. We had to study the geography of the European and Pacific theaters to learn the supply lines and the distance between bases and targets. We had to learn about how missions were organized—how fighters and bombers came together to wreak havoc on our foes.

We were not regular students. We had to wear uniforms and maintain military discipline. While we took our meals at Harvard, we could not just walk to the cafeteria—we had to march. Each day, one of us would act as the drill sergeant, calling the others to attention and ordering them about as if we were on a military base instead of the on the campus of an Ivy League school. Wherever we went, we were always singing a song about the Air Forces and trying to sing it louder than the navy men who were there at the same time.

The Harvard program was a crash course; they worked us from early in the morning to late at night five days a week and gave us homework on top of that. The professors said we learned more in two months than their regular students learned in two years. Of course, we had some real motivation to succeed. We were all scared to death that if we failed, we wouldn't get commissioned and would end up in a foxhole somewhere, so we all worked like hell.

After we graduated, a tailor came in and fitted us all for our new uniforms. We were now second lieutenants in the U.S. Army Air Forces. A few days later, I got orders to report to Wright Field in Dayton, Ohio.

>✧<✧<

Wright Field was the headquarters of the Air Materiel Command.[6] There was a huge IBM installation at the base—the largest in the world—

---

6 In August 1944, it was integrated with the previously separate Air Services Command to form the Air Technical Services Command. See USAF *Historical Division, The Army Air Forces*

and I was given the job of running it from midnight to eight in the morning. The primary purpose of that installation was to keep track of all the aircraft that were grounded and awaiting parts all over the world. Our job was to make sure they got back in the air as quickly as possible. That mostly meant expediting the shipment of necessary parts from distribution centers in the United States and overseas. We also controlled the parts inventory for the Air Forces.

We had some really good enlisted men who, in civilian life, had been IBM supervisors. We also had a skilled civilian staff. These guys knew what they were doing. If there was a problem, we would sit down together and figure out how to solve it as a team. We did not pay much attention to rank but handled things largely as we would have outside in the business world. I also served as a liaison with IBM, resolving the inevitable disputes that arose between the company and military personnel. After three months, I was promoted to first lieutenant. Three months after that, I was reassigned to the day shift.

My commanding officer was Major Francis Reith. Everybody called him Jack. He was a great guy—very personable and energetic, with a great personality. He was very outgoing, and soon we were friends, too.

At the end of the year, I was promoted to captain and reassigned to a top-secret project with the code name "QQ Movement." My job was to reorganize and supervise the IBM installations at the three in-transit supply depots responsible for shipping parts to airfields in Asia and the Pacific to support the new B-29 heavy bombers that were preparing to launch Operation Matterhorn: the aerial offensive against the Japanese home islands.[7]

The three depots—located in Long Beach and Oakland in California and in Tacoma, Washington—were having some trouble. The punch

in World War II Volume VI: Men and Planes, W.F. Craven and J.L. Cate, editors (Chicago: The University of Chicago Press, 1955), pp.64-65.

7 Though the B-29 Superfortress entered service in late 1943, the first bombers only arrived at airfields in India and China in April 1944, entering combat for the first time on June 5 when ninety-eight planes bombed the Japanese rail yards in Bangkok, Thailand. This was the beginning of Operation Matterhorn. The first raid against the Japanese home islands themselves took place ten days later, when sixty-eight B-29s took off from China to bomb the Imperial Iron and Steel Works on the island of Kyushu.

cards were not being entered correctly, and the data wasn't being checked against the actual records. To make matters worse, the staff was not properly trained and some of the machines were wired incorrectly. It was a big mess. The lack of parts for our bombers was limiting their operations, and I was sent out to the West Coast to sort it out.

It took months, but I finally managed to get everything running smoothly and received a glowing letter of commendation from the commander out there:

Captain Chase Morsey Jr., Army serial number 0649991, was assigned to this section on temporary duty. By clear thinking and the application of principles of good management, and a great deal of plain physical energy, he had placed the operation of this vital branch on a current basis. The services of Captain Morsey were of great value to the section during a very critical period.

A few months after I returned to Wright Field, Reith was transferred, and Robert McNamara became my new commanding officer. He put me in charge of the whole IBM installation.

I watched the war unfold from my office in Dayton. If a new squadron of bombers was needed somewhere in the Pacific, we would assemble it from the lists of aircraft and personnel that we maintained at Wright Field and prepare the necessary orders to move those men and machines to where they were needed. Yet we were also detached from the outcomes of these movements. We had no insight into the action itself; we only learned the results from reading the newspaper. But it was still very exciting. We knew we were keeping our planes and pilots in the air. We knew we were making a difference, and after a few months, I was promoted to major.

One day, as I was talking with some of my team members, someone threw open the door and shouted, "The war's over!" We were all thrilled and relieved, but we had to stick around for several more months to help Uncle Sam clean up the mess.

In April 1946 I returned to St. Louis and went back to work for IBM. Having proved myself in New Haven, I was excited to be home and working out of a bigger office. I got to handle some of IBM's most important accounts in the city: General Motors, Carter Carburetor, McDonnell Aircraft, Bell Telephone, and the War Department.

Business was booming, but I soon became bored. The whole time I was in the service, I had never even thought about doing anything else, yet I was ready for a new challenge. When the president of the Dazey Products Company offered me a job as his assistant, I accepted it on the spot. I was eager for the chance to gain more managerial experience.

Dazey manufactured home appliances, and working there afforded me the opportunity to learn about manufacturing and the retail business. I was put in charge of overseeing the launch of the company's first new product in ten years. It was an eggbeater, and I was responsible for coordinating the efforts of the chief engineer, the purchasing director, the product control manager, and the new product development manager.

It was a success, and I was soon offered a job by the D.E. Sanford Company, which handled national sales for Dazey. Seeing this as an opportunity to learn about yet another facet of business, I accepted and was soon made district sales manager. I really enjoyed that job, as it allowed me to get out into the field and deal directly with the big wholesalers and department stores that purchased our products. In addition to training and managing the sales team responsible for six midwestern states, I got to go into the big chain stores, set up the displays, and check on their inventories.

Then one day in late 1948, I received a telephone call from my old army buddy Jack Reith. He told me that he and several of the other officers from Statistical Control had gone to work for the Ford Motor Company. Reith said he knew how much I loved Fords and asked if I would be interested in joining them in Dearborn.

He didn't have to ask me twice.

Chapter Two

A BINDER FULL
OF BLUNDER

The Ford Motor Company was founded by the great industrialist Henry Ford in 1903. Henry Ford did not invent the automobile, but he did transform it from an expensive toy into a means of transportation—one accessible to people of every social class. In doing so, Ford became the company that put the world on wheels. Ford did invent the moving assembly line and create the industrial class that would become the foundation of American prosperity for much of the twentieth century. He also created the industrial system that would allow America to win two world wars. By the time I arrived at Ford's headquarters in Dearborn, Michigan, in 1948, the company's name had become synonymous with progress. But the truth was that Ford was fighting for its life.

It had been for some time.

After Henry Ford launched his famous Model T in 1908, the Ford Motor Company quickly became the largest automobile manufacturer in the world. But Ford had competition. Its biggest competitor was the General Motors Corporation—a collection of brands that William Durant began assembling that same year.

While Henry Ford believed his Model T was the only car people needed, General Motors offered different models aimed at different consumer demographics, from the everyman's Chevrolet to the upscale

Cadillac for the well-to-do. Henry Ford grudgingly added Lincoln[8] to his stable in 1922, but by then General Motors had half a dozen different brands. And most of GM's brands introduced new models every few years, while Ford's Model T remained largely unchanged. By 1927, Ford's sales were in a nose-dive. Finally convinced of the need for something new, Henry Ford closed his factories to retool for the Model A. That was all the opening General Motors needed, and it blew past Ford to become the largest automaker in the world.

Ford would never regain that title, but it would sure give GM a run for its money. When the Model A was finally unveiled, it proved just as popular as the Model T had been in its heyday. Ford's market share doubled in just two years, accounting for nearly a third of all the cars built in America. By 1930, the company's share of the market hit 41 percent.

But the Great Depression took a heavy toll on winners and losers alike. By 1932, Ford's production had fallen to levels not seen since the eve of World War I. Then Henry Ford turned the industry on its head once again by introducing the flathead V-8 engine. The V-8 put Ford at the forefront of the automobile industry once again, at least as far as speed enthusiasts were concerned, and revived the automaker's fortunes in the midst of the Great Depression. And while General Motors had become too large for the Ford Motor Company to overcome, the new engine allowed the Ford brand to blow past Chevrolet and reclaim the title of best-selling brand in America.[9] Ford made other important changes as well. The company finally started introducing new models every year, just like General Motors and the rest of its competitors. That gave Ford's designers a chance to show the world what they could do. Ford's cars became longer and sleeker, and Ford kept boosting the power of its V-8 to make sure they remained among the fastest.

But Henry Ford continued to resist innovation in other areas. He stubbornly refused to adopt the much more effective hydraulic brakes

---

8   The Lincoln Motor Company was founded by Henry Leland in 1917 and purchased by Ford in 1922.

9   Chevrolet would take that crown back a couple of years later but not for long. It soon belonged to Ford again, and the two brands are still fighting over it today.

that were proving so popular with GM customers. He wanted nothing to do with independent front suspension or counterbalanced hoods either.[10] And he continued to balk at his archrival's brand strategy.

By the mid-1930s, General Motors not only had a brand for every consumer demographic but also a full line of cars for each brand. The Ford Motor Company just had Ford and Lincoln, and each of those had a limited lineup. As the economy faltered again in 1939, Henry Ford's son, Edsel, finally persuaded his father to add a third midmarket brand—Mercury. But it was too late. General Motors had widened the gap, and Ford's fortunes were foundering once again.

Just when it seemed like the company was headed for real trouble, World War II began. By 1940, Ford was producing aircraft engines. The company introduced its first six-cylinder motor since 1907 in 1941, offering a cheaper alternative to the powerful V-8. But civilian automobile production halted in February 1942. For the next three years, Ford and the other American automakers would only produce military vehicles.

Like the rest of Detroit, Ford would become an important part of what President Franklin Roosevelt dubbed the "Arsenal of Democracy." So important, in fact, that the War Department was not willing to leave the company in the hands of an aging and increasingly eccentric Henry Ford. After Edsel died in 1943, Washington panicked. Henry Ford's oldest grandson, Henry Ford II, was serving in the U.S. Navy. He was ordered back to Dearborn and told to take over the corporation. It took some doing, but old Henry finally relented.[11]

The company that Henry Ford II inherited was in disarray. His grandfather's cronies and hangers-on were running the show with little accountability. There were no modern business practices in place. The Finance Department only knew how much money it had by checking the bank statements, and it estimated monthly expenses by weighing the pile of bills. Henry Ford II, or "Hank the Deuce," as he soon became

---

10 Ford finally added hydraulic brakes to its 1939 models.

11 Henry Ford II was released from the navy to become the vice president of Ford Motor Company in December 1943. He became president of the company in September 1945. Henry Ford himself died in 1947 at the age of eighty-three.

known, sacked his grandfather's henchman and demanded full account-ability from all of his managers. But when the war ended, he was still struggling to reorganize the company.

Demand for new cars and trucks exploded once civilian produc-tion resumed in 1945. Ford started building the same uncompetitive products it had been building before the war, but it initially outsold Chevrolet. However, General Motors quickly rushed refreshed models to the market, while Ford kept tweaking the same old car. Soon half of all the cars sold in America came from one of GM's brands, while Ford sank back into the red. The company was losing $10 million a month.[12] Henry Ford II knew he needed help. He knew he needed men beside him who knew how to run a car company. So, in 1946, he approached one of GM's top executives, Ernie Breech, and asked him to help save the Ford Motor Company.

Breech was a tough, dynamic leader with a solid financial back-ground and a reputation as a talented problem-solver. He had rescued the North American Aviation Company in the 1930s and was then serving as president of GM's Bendix Aviation Division.[13] Breech accepted Ford's challenge. He resigned from GM in July 1946 and came to Dearborn. But he didn't come alone.

Breech brought several other GM executives with him, including Harold Youngren, formerly the chief engineer at Oldsmobile; Earle MacPherson, formerly the chief design engineer at Chevrolet; and Delmar Harder, one of GM's brightest manufacturing experts. But his most important new recruit for Ford was Lewis Crusoe, formerly the controller of GM's Fisher Body Division. Crusoe had already retired once from General Motors, but Breech had convinced him to return to Bendix. Crusoe came to Ford as Breech's special assistant but was soon promoted to vice president of Finance.

---

12 David Halberstam, *The Reckoning* (New York: William Morrow and Company, 1986), p. 99. The actual figure may have been much higher from what I heard.
13 Douglas Brinkley, *Wheels for the World: Henry Ford, His Company and a Century of Progress* (New York: Viking Penguin, 2003), p. 501.

Together, these men transformed Ford from a seat-of-the-pants start-up company into a modern corporation. It was nothing revolutionary—they just implemented the same sort of practices and procedures that General Motors had been following for decades. It worked, but Breech and the other GM executives also brought a lot of prejudices and preconceived notions of how to make and sell automobiles with them. That was fine with Henry Ford II; if they remade his company in GM's image, at least it would become a profitable enterprise once again. The respective market shares of the two companies was all the proof they needed to convince Ford that GM's way was the right way.

Breech and the other GM veterans were not the only new hires Henry Ford II made. After the war, my former superiors in Statistical Control decided to hire themselves out to corporate America. They knew that the methods they had pioneered and perfected in the U.S. Army Air Forces had the potential to transform the way companies did business. After the war, Colonel Charles "Tex" Thornton, the commander of Statistical Control in Washington, contacted scores of corporations, offering his services and those of the nine other senior officers who ran the unit. It was an all-or-none proposition, the whole team or no one.

Thornton sent a telegram to the Ford Motor Company on October 19, 1945. "I would like to see you regarding a subject which I believe would be of immediate interest," he wrote to Henry Ford II. "This concerns a system which has been developed and applied successfully in the management of the Army Air Forces for the past three years."

Desperate for help sorting out the mess that he had inherited, the young Ford summoned Thornton to Dearborn the next day. Within a few weeks, Ford had agreed to hire Thornton and his associates: Wilbur Andreson; Charles Bosworth; J. Edward Lundy; Arjay Miller; Ben Mills; George Moore; James Wright, who had recruited me for Statistical Control in Miami Beach; my former commander, Robert McNamara; and my old pal, Jack Reith. They would spend the next couple of years dragging Ford out of the Dark Ages and figuring out how to apply what we had learned fighting the Germans and Japanese to the car and truck business.

—◇—

Thornton and his team had already been dubbed the "Whiz Kids" by the time Reith called me in the fall of 1948. I was at home in Clayton, a suburb of St. Louis. I had gotten married about a year before. My wife's name was Mary Ann. She was from St. Louis. I met her at a debutante party after the war. We were just beginning to build a life for ourselves in Missouri when Reith asked me to drop everything and come to Michigan.

"Come on up here," Jack said. "You'll enjoy it. I've got a job I think you'll be interested in."

I accepted immediately. I was so excited by the prospect of going to work for the Ford Motor Company that I forgot to ask him what the job was! I just heard the word "Ford," and that was good enough for me. The word itself was magical. Plus, Jack was a good friend, and I trusted him. It just felt right.

Mary Ann's family was a little less enthusiastic. They understood why I wanted to go to work for a big automaker like Ford, but they did not relish the idea of us moving to Michigan and leaving St. Louis society. But this was a dream come true for me, and that was all there was to it. I loaded up my Ford and set out for Dearborn.

On a cold day in November, I checked into the Dearborn Inn—a redbrick hotel close to Ford's headquarters. I met Reith there the next day. When Jack showed me to my desk, I realized that I probably should have asked him some questions before taking the job. I was not given an office. Jack didn't have one either. But I also learned that I was not on the bonus roll, nor would I be eating in the executive dining room. I would have to stand in line in the cafeteria, just like in the army. My title was budget analyst. Jack was the manager of Ford's budget office, and I would be reporting to him. A Finance position was not exactly what I'd had in mind when I accepted his offer. I thought I would be working on cars! And it only got worse.

Reith led me to a large room. The walls were lined with big forty-by sixty-inch boards covered with numbers. He explained that the company was in the process of putting together its annual budget for 1949. The details were laid out on these boards. More than half a dozen budget analysts were seated at desks around the room, hammering away on adding machines. Jack asked me to check the numbers on the boards against their numbers.

I got to work, assuming it was just something he wanted me to do until he had time to go over my full responsibilities. After a few hours, one of the other men asked to carry some of the boards over to the Graphic Arts Department across the street so that they could change or amend them. I soon found myself toting a hefty stack of boards down a dark tunnel that ran beneath Schaeffer Boulevard between the two buildings. When I arrived on the other side, I was relieved of my burden and handed another pile to take back to the budget office. When I returned, there were more boards waiting to be proofed; then I received another call asking me to take those over to the meeting room. And the cycle just kept repeating itself. After several weeks of this monotony, I went looking for Reith.

"Jack, what the hell am I doing here?" I whispered, taking him aside. "Why do you have me carrying these boards around and not working on Fords?"

Reith smiled. "Just be patient," he said.

⤜⤛⤜⤛

Despite the efforts of the General Motors men and the Whiz Kids to remake the Ford Motor Company, the situation had gone from bad to worse. Ford was now the number three automaker in the United States, having ceded second place to the Chrysler Corporation. The company was betting everything on its all-new 1949 model. The car was beautifully styled. It was slab-sided, one of the first American car without fenders. But it was poorly engineered, and it was rushed into production, so the quality suffered. The first ones off the line were real lemons. The doors, hood, and trunk fit poorly, so the car would leak when it rained. If you drove it down a dusty road, the trunk would fill up with dirt. There were problems with the seat cushions. The front suspension was weak and would break if the car went over certain types of railroad crossings. But the '49 Ford looked so good that people still lined up to buy them.

I returned to St. Louis to spend Christmas with Mary Ann and then brought her back to Michigan in January 1949. We found a house to rent in Grosse Pointe through a college friend of hers who lived there. As soon as I returned to work, Reith called me into his office. I knew something was up, because Jack had been sitting out on the floor with the rest of the guys, like me. Now he had an office of his own with a secretary out front, and he was grinning when she showed me in.

"Well, Chase, we're no longer in the budget office," Jack told me. "We now work for the Ford Division. I'm chief of staff, and you're manager of product planning."

"Great!" I said. "What's that?"

Reith explained that Ford was in the middle of a great transformation. While General Motors had separate divisions for each of its brands, Ford had been run as one big conglomerate. The same engineering department was responsible for everything from luxury Lincolns to workaday Ford trucks. The same went for design, purchasing, and every other part of the business. But Breech and his GM associates were in the process of changing that. They were dividing the once-centralized company up into separate divisions in order to drive accountability and maximize profits.

The Ford brand itself constituted one of these new divisions. Reith and several of the other Whiz Kids had been given key positions in the Ford Division, and as they put together the organization chart, they had realized that no one person had ultimate responsibility for the car itself. In the past, there had been little coordination between the different functions that were responsible for designing, building, and selling Ford vehicles. The Manufacturing Department simply built the car the Engineering Department designed, and it was up to the Sales Department to sell it.

The Whiz Kids wanted to foster more cooperation among these different groups, and they wanted there to be one person with the overall responsibility of coordinating their efforts. So they decided to create a new department called "Product Planning," and they wanted me to run it.[14] I would be responsible for all future product plans, from the design phase to sales and marketing. But I would start with Ford's next big thing. Reith slid a thick black binder across his desk.

"Now here's the plan for the '52 Ford car," he said. "It's going to be your job to monitor this. I mean, the decisions have all been made by all the top executives, but you've got to follow through and see that it's executed. You've got to work with Styling, Engineering, and Manufacturing. You've got to work with the Sales Department and Finance. You've got to coordinate all that stuff for the Ford Division. It's all written up here. Mr. Ford and Mr. Breech just approved this last week. Take it home, and familiarize yourself with it. The future of the company is riding on this car, and it's your job to make sure that it's a success. Take it home over the weekend, and we'll talk about it Monday morning."

I was thrilled. I was finally going to be working on Ford's cars! No more toting around budget boards for me! I looked at the book. It was entitled "The Forward Plan for the Ford Car."

Now, that's more like it! I thought as I grabbed my coat and headed for the door. I couldn't stop smiling all the way home. I could hardly wait to get started! After dinner, I took the book into my study and began leafing through it.

It was filled with a lot of technical information that was pretty incomprehensible to me at the time. But I could see that the '52 Ford would be a big improvement over the cars the company was making at the time. It would have a longer wheelbase and sleek, aerodynamic styling. I was getting pretty excited about the whole thing, until I started reading the section on power trains. There was no mention of a V-8! The plan only called for a six-cylinder engine! I almost had a heart attack.

---

14 General Motors and Chrysler would later see the value of this function and create their own product planning departments.

There's no V-8!? You've got to be kidding me!

I thought back to all my trips across the country between Amherst and St. Louis in my Fords. I thought about the gas-station attendants and how they would grin when they lifted up my hood and saw that big engine. I thought about all the other motorists who had looked longingly at my Ford and asked, "Do you have a V-8 in there?" I knew Ford enthusiasts. I was one of them. And I knew that to them, the V-8 *was* the Ford car. And now Ford was getting ready to get rid of it.

Ford doesn't know what the hell they're doing! I thought. *This is going to cost me my job!*

Chapter Three

NINETY DAYS THAT SAVED FORD

T he V-8 engine was originally developed by French aircraft designer and inventor Léon Levavasseur in 1902 for use in airplanes and racing boats. It would be three years before anyone thought of putting such a powerful motor in an automobile, but when they did that car set a new land-speed record.[15] Rolls-Royce introduced the first commercially available V-8 automobile later in 1905 but only sold three of them. Cadillac switched to V-8 engines in 1914, taking the engine mainstream—at least for luxury automobiles.

For most automobile enthusiasts, the V-8 was only something to dream about. But Henry Ford changed all that in 1932. Just as he had done with the automobile itself, Ford figured out how to make them cheaper and better. Ford cast the crankcase and all eight cylinders together in a single block, greatly reducing the cost and improving the reliability of the powerful motor. It was Henry Ford's last great engineering innovation, and it allowed his company to offer a V-8 option in the '32 Ford for just fifty dollars more than the base four-cylinder model.

Ford's flathead V-8 was an immediate hit with anyone who loved speed. As you will recall, I was one of them. The first time I saw one

---

15 That car, built by French automaker Automobiles Darracq S.A. specifically for that purpose, still exists.

of those V-8 Fords zoom by, it turned my head. I knew that was what I wanted to drive. And I was not alone. More than 5 million Americans turned out to see the new V-8 Ford the week it was launched. As the historian Douglas Brinkley wrote in his seminal work on the Ford Motor Company, *Wheels for the World*, "By 1934 the Ford V-8 had developed its own legion of enthusiasts. Henry Ford received many letters of unabashed praise for the company's accomplishment from kings, presidents, schoolchildren and even gangsters."

The notorious John Dillinger—known then as "Public Enemy Number One"—was one of them.

"Hello, Old Pal," he wrote in a letter dated May 16, 1934. "You have a wonderful car. Been driving it for three weeks. It's a treat to drive one. Your slogan should be: Drive a Ford and watch the other cars fall behind you. I can make any other car take a Ford's dust."

Clyde Barrow offered his own praise for the V-8.

"While I still have got breath in my lungs I will tell you what a dandy car you make," he wrote to Henry Ford. "I have drove Fords exclusively when I could get away with one. For sustained speed and freedom from trouble the Ford has got every other car skinned and even if my business hasn't been strictly legal it don't hurt anything to tell you what a fine car you got in the V-8."

With so many outlaws driving Ford V-8s, police departments all over America began buying them too, just to keep up. Two-door Ford coupes and roadsters became the cars everyone who wanted to go fast dreamed about.[16] But it wasn't just speed demons who loved the V-8. The powerful motor was also adored by Ford's pickup customers, who valued its torque, as well as its impressive towing and hauling capabilities. And pickup trucks were becoming an increasingly important part of the automobile landscape in postwar America.

Chevrolet had nothing to match the V-8. That was why I had stuck with Fords, and it was why a lot of other Americans had, too. Chevys

---

16 The 1932 Ford Coupe—or "Deuce Coupe" as it was later known—would later become the most popular car for hot-rodders.

might have had hydraulic brakes, but only a Ford had a V-8. And I was determined to make sure it stayed that way, even if it cost me my job.

I spent the whole weekend reading and rereading every page of that black book. The plan was even worse than it first appeared. Not only was the Ford Motor Company going to eliminate the V-8 engine as an option on the 1952 Ford car, it was going to kill it entirely. That meant it would no longer be an option for the company's pickup trucks either.

At that point, Ford customers had the choice of either a V-8 or an old L-head six. For the 1952 model year, both would be replaced by a new overhead-valve six-cylinder motor. This new engine looked a lot like the "Stovebolt Six" that had powered all Chevrolet cars since 1937.[17] This new motor would be the sole engine for all Ford cars and light trucks. Over the next two years, all but one of the company's V-8 assembly lines were to be converted to production of the new six.

Though I strongly disagreed with this decision, I quickly understood how Ford's senior executives had arrived at it. The new six *was* a more modern design, and each part of the company had its own reasons for supporting the single-engine strategy.

For the Engineering Department, it was all a matter of efficiency. All else being equal, a six-cylinder engine weighed less, was simpler to manufacture, and usually burned less fuel than a V-8. A smaller motor also generated less heat, which meant it could be cooled by a smaller, less expensive radiator.[18] The lighter weight of the six-cylinder would also allow the company to use less beefy engine mounts and lighter frame members, springs, shock absorbers, steering gears, brakes, wheels, and

---

17 Chevrolet's OHV six was first introduced in 1929, but it was extensively redesigned for the 1937 model year. The new Ford engine's resemblance to the Chevrolet motor was noted by critics.

18 In 1952, Ford's flathead V-8 required a twenty-two-quart radiator, while the new OHV six used a much smaller seventeen-quart unit. See Tim Howley, "SIA Comparison Report: The New and the Old: 1952 Ford Six vs. V8," *Special Interest Autos* No. 143 (September–October 1994). The six also needed only a single water pump, where the flathead V-8 had two; see *Mechanic's Handbook 1949-Ford Passenger Cars 'V-8' and '6'* (Dearborn: Ford Motor Company, 1948), pp. 13–14.

even tires. Added together, the potential weight savings could amount to hundreds of pounds per car, translating into better fuel economy, easier handling, and superior performance, even with a smaller, less powerful engine. The fact that Ford's all-new overhead-valve six was actually a bit more powerful than the existing flathead V-8 was icing on the cake.

Manufacturing and Purchasing had even more reason to rejoice about the elimination of the V-8. Offering both a six and a V-8 had meant buying and maintaining two distinct sets of tooling (dies, molds, jigs, and so forth) and two separate stockpiles of parts. Offering a single engine promised to streamline assembly operations, simplify logistics, and even improve quality control on the final assembly line, where workers would only have one engine to worry about.

The potential for improved quality convinced Ford's sales organization to support the decision as well. Sales saw it as a way to appease dealers, who had been complaining for months about the poor quality of the '49 Ford. Sales also hoped the money saved would be spent on other areas that customers could see and touch, such as upholstery and trim. They figured most dealers and car buyers couldn't care less about how many cylinders there were under the hood, but they had not bothered to poll them to find out if that was really the case.

Back then Ford and the other automakers thought it was their job to design and build the cars and the dealers' job to sell them. Ford did have a Dealer Council made up of elected representatives of franchise holders from each region of the country. However, while those representatives could and did offer feedback and complaints, the council seldom had an opportunity to do so until after a new product was introduced to the market. To the extent that the company anticipated dealer resistance to the loss of the V-8, it was assumed that such concerns could be countered with advertising and promotional materials emphasizing the six's superior power and gas mileage.

Of course, the biggest reason for Ford's decision to adopt a six-cylinder-only engine strategy was because the same strategy had worked so well for Chevrolet. At General Motors, only midmarket brands, such as Pontiac and Oldsmobile, offered a choice of either a six- or eight-cylinder engine, and the men in charge in Dearborn were almost all GM veterans.[19] Henry Ford II had hired them to remake Ford in GM's image, so it only made sense that they would want to adopt the same powertrain strategy.

After all, General Motors was successful, and Ford was losing money. GM was making big profits and selling more cars without a V-8, so why spend all the extra money offering one if it was not helping the bottom line? For the former General Motors executives now running the company, the V-8 seemed like a needless extravagance. The six-cylinder-only formula had worked well for Chevrolet since 1929; there was no reason to think it would not do just as well for Ford.

The argument seemed even more compelling when it came to trucks. In those days, pickups were primarily purchased for business, and price and economy of operation were paramount considerations. Chevrolet was the leader in truck sales, too, even though it did not offer an eight-cylinder engine—even in its heavy trucks, nor did GMC, Dodge, or International, the other major pickup manufacturers.

Given all of this, dropping the V-8 no doubt seemed so logical and obvious to Breech and the other former GM guys that they spent little time studying whether or not it was the correct decision. The idea that it might be a mistake from a marketing or sales standpoint was never seriously considered. Such unshakeable confidence was emblematic of the GM mentality that now pervaded Ford headquarters. The idea that GM's approach to Chevrolet might not work for the Ford brand was unthinkable.

But I knew they were wrong—not about the benefits of the new six-cylinder engine but about the impact that killing the V-8 would have on Ford's brand image.

I knew it because I *was* a Ford customer, and I had been one for years. For men like me, the V-8 engine was synonymous with the Ford

---

19 Breech and the other GM men figured that the Mercury brand would fill that niche at Ford.

car itself. And it was men like me that were keeping the Ford Motor Company in business. We bought Fords not because they made more sense from an engineering or manufacturing point of view but because they represented something more than mere transportation. I knew that a Chevrolet could get me from my home to work just as well as any Ford, but that big V-8 under the hood kept me from ever thinking about switching brands.

For me, buying a car was different from buying a toaster. It was a deeply emotional and personal experience. And I knew that many other customers felt the same way. Without a V-8, customers' whole reason for choosing a Ford instead of a Chevrolet would be gone. The truth was that many Ford customers cared very deeply about how many cylinders there were under the hood, but nobody in Dearborn had thought to ask for their opinion.

In those days, customers were not consulted about future products. That was the case not only at Ford, but across the industry. The attitude was, "They will buy what we tell them to buy." It was arrogant, and I knew intuitively that it was wrong. My experience at IBM had shown me the importance of catering to the needs and desires of the customer. If that worked for selling business machines, I reckoned it would certainly work for selling something as emotionally charged as an automobile.

I wrestled with myself all weekend. I knew that killing the V-8 would be a disaster for Ford. While I could understand how the company's top management had come to that decision, I knew that they were missing the big picture. But what could I do about it? Jack Reith had told me that the '52 Ford program had already been approved by all the senior executives—including Mr. Ford himself. If I told them they were wrong, I might find myself out on the street. I figured that I could always go back to IBM if that happened, but I was still really frightened about the prospect of being fired. In the end, I decided that I cared too much about Ford to keep my mouth shut.

I was waiting for Reith when he arrived at the office Monday morning.

"Jack, this damn thing will break the Ford Motor Company!" I exclaimed. "This is just stupid!"

I went over all the reasons why it did not make sense to get rid of the vaunted V-8.

"Jack, you know that—during the war—you and I talked about cars a lot. You knew I loved Fords, and you knew that I knew a lot about Ford cars. Jack, the V-8 *is* the Ford car," I said. "This engine is the only advantage that we've got over Chevrolet, as far as I can see. This is just wrong! I didn't see anything in your book that talked about the dealers or the customers, but I can tell you that they're not going to be happy about this. If we drop the V-8 engine and become just like Chevrolet, what in the world will our dealers have to sell, except the name *Ford*?"

"But, Chase, they had this big meeting of the Product Planning Committee. All the top executives were there. And they all agreed that this was the way Ford should go. The V-8 costs too much money. It requires us to have double tooling. Without the V-8, we'll be able to cut costs and maybe start making a profit," Reith said. "Everyone in the company is behind this plan, so this *is* the plan!"

I kept at him.

"Jack, you keep telling me that Henry keeps saying that we need to beat Chevrolet," I said. "How are we going to do that without the V-8?"

Reith just sat there listening with his mouth open. I could see he was already regretting his decision to bring me to Dearborn. But I kept going until I had spoken my mind, and I could tell that at least some of what I was telling him made sense. Jack knew me from the war. He had not only been my friend but also my commanding officer. He trusted me, and he knew how much I cared about the Ford Motor Company. That was why he had hired me.

"OK," Reith sighed when I finally shut up. "I guess I better go see Crusoe."

Like Ernest Breech, Lewis Crusoe believed General Motors had already figured out the automobile business, and he had little time for the Whiz Kids—except when their methods advanced his cause of transforming Ford into a modern corporation and enforcing financial discipline throughout the organization. Crusoe was now head of the newly formed Ford Division, the man with overall responsibility for Ford's cars and trucks. He was also Reith's boss.

Just as I realized what a spot I had put my friend in, Jack returned.

"Crusoe wants to talk to you," he said. "Follow me."

I was more than a little nervous as I walked down the hall to Crusoe's office. Jack knew me. We were friends. If I spoke my mind to him, it was only because I knew he would hear me out and take what I had to say seriously. But I had never met Crusoe before. To him, I was just some new hire, fresh off the street, with no experience in the automotive industry. I was not sure if I was even going to get a chance to make my case—he might have just been calling me in to fire me. As I approached his office, I figured there was a good chance my career at the Ford Motor Company might be ending right then and there.

I swallowed hard as Reith knocked on the door and motioned for me to enter. Crusoe sat behind a large desk. He was a scholarly looking man, with thick glasses and a piercing stare. He looked highly intelligent and reminded me a bit of old Dean Porter. But I was here to ask for a bit more than a little flexibility in the restrictions on underclassmen owning automobiles.

Crusoe wasted no time getting to the point.

"You've only been at this company for six weeks," he said sternly. "Why do you think that this program the rest of us have approved is wrong?"

"Mr. Crusoe, I may have only been at the Ford Motor Company for six weeks, but I've been a Ford owner for thirteen years. And, with all respect, I did not find anything in this presentation that talked about customers or dealers or their preferences," I said, holding up the black book. "I know that the Ford dealers and the Ford customers love the Ford V-8 the same way I love it. It is what makes a Ford car a Ford car—and it's the only advantage that we have against Chevrolet. If we only offer a six, then we'll be just like Chevrolet, and we'll have nothing more to offer customers than the name *Ford*. As you know, Chevrolet has a much stronger dealer organization. They've been the industry leader for years. We'll never be able to compete, much less beat them. The only way we can do that is with the V-8!"

Crusoe listened in silence, betraying no hint of what he thought of my increasingly impassioned monologue. Finally, he raised his hand, and I shut up.

"Young man, how old are you?" he asked.

"Mr. Crusoe, I'm twenty-nine years old," I said.

"And how long have you been working in the automobile industry?"

"Six weeks, sir."

"So you've never worked for any other automaker?"

"No, sir."

"Don't you think you're a little young and inexperienced to be making such strong statements, when everybody—*all* the *top* executives of the Ford Motor Company—have approved this plan?"

"Yes, Mr. Crusoe. But you will kill the Ford dealers if you take away the V-8. The V-8 *is* the Ford car."

"Why are you so sure?"

"Because I've driven my Ford all over this country. When I was in college, I used to drive it back and forth between Amherst and St. Louis several times each year. And every time I stopped for gasoline, the service-station attendants would come up to me and say, 'Boy, you've got that V-8 engine!' If I had any problem with my car and took it into the Ford dealership, the conversation always came around to the V-8. Everybody always wanted to talk to me about that motor. That's part of the reason I love my Ford so much—and I know that most of the other Ford customers feel the same way as I do."

"Well, I don't know," said Crusoe hesitantly.

I could see I was beginning to get through to him. It was a small opening, but I decided to take it.

"Look, Mr. Crusoe, I have nothing to prove it to you with right now. But if you just give me ninety days to set up a market research department, I will go out and *get* the proof."

"Hmmm," Crusoe said. "I always wondered why Chevrolet didn't have a V-8."

I smiled. But Crusoe frowned.

"I guess I'll have to go see Mr. Breech," he sighed. "I don't think he's going to be very happy about this. We just approved the plan. But I'll see what he says."

Crusoe got up and left Reith and me in his office. At least this time, I didn't have to sweat it out alone. But Jack just sat there, staring at me like I was crazy.

"Well, you made your case pretty strong," he said.

"I hope I didn't make it too strong," I said.

Jack just shook his head.

Maybe I was crazy to have spoken to Crusoe like that. He was one of the most powerful men in the Ford Motor Company—a veteran of the automobile business before he ever set foot in the building. I was just a new hire, too young and inexperienced to know when to keep my mouth shut. But I was also a die-hard Ford fan, and I felt like it had fallen to me to speak up for all of the other Ford enthusiasts out there on the highways and byways of America. I was already beginning to regret it though, when Crusoe returned. He did not look pleased.

"As I predicted, Mr. Breech was not happy," Crusoe said. "He said it would be like an earthquake shaking the company if we were to tear up this whole plan and start over now that we've just approved it."

I thought about IBM and hoped I was right about still being welcome there.

"But he gave you ninety days," Crusoe said. "So, get to work!"

I was numb when I walked out of Crusoe's office. I was glad that I had gotten their attention, but I knew that I had really put myself on the spot.

Now I have to prove it! I thought.

I was determined to do just that. I believed every word that I had said to Crusoe, and I was confident that the facts would back them up. To that end, I started assembling a market-research study. I wanted to talk to Ford dealers, Ford customers, and even Chevrolet owners. My new position at the company was not very well defined, so I decided that my job was to be the advocate for all of them. I had an office and a secretary now but no staff. Nothing like this had been done at Ford before. The company did have a guy on staff who did what they called market research—asking people what they thought of the Ford Motor Company and whether or not they liked the company's advertising. Frankly, I thought that was a bunch of nonsense. What I wanted to do was really get at what our customers wanted and valued. Such research may be routine today, but questions such as these were not asked in those days—at least not in the automobile industry. However, they were second nature to me, because they were just the sorts of questions I had asked prospective customers in my former job at IBM. So I asked Ford's researcher to help me design a study. We were still formulating the questions that would be asked when Crusoe called me and asked me to come to his office again.

"Finance thinks that the V-8 costs one helluva lot more than the six to make," he told me. "They think that's why we're not making any money."

He showed me a report that the bean counters had prepared that showed the V-8 engine cost the company one hundred dollars more to produce than the six-cylinder motor. I knew enough about manufacturing to know that was ridiculous.

"Well, Mr. Crusoe, it's only got two more cylinders," I said. "It *can't* cost one hundred dollars more."

Crusoe nodded in agreement.

"Look, Chase, I've got a friend over in central staff in Manufacturing, away from Finance's cost department," he said. "You should go over and see him, and ask him to process a modern overhead-valve V-8 with a modern overhead-valve six to see what is the true cost difference between the two of them."

I agreed. The man's name was Roy T. Hurley.[20] He was one of Ford's biggest manufacturing experts. And he was quite enthusiastic about the idea. Hurley explained that automatic-transfer equipment was just becoming available, which would allow Ford to bore the cylinder holes in the engine blocks by machine, rather than by hand. He said that would result in huge savings of both time and money, greatly reducing the cost differential between the two motors. I asked him to run the numbers.

Meanwhile, I hired a market-research firm to go out and talk to customers and do the actual interviews. They asked people what they thought of the V-8 engine, whether they would still buy a Ford if it did not have a V-8, and how much more they would be willing to pay for a V-8. Just as I predicted, most people felt strongly about the motor and said it was a major factor in their decision to purchase a Ford car. But even I was surprised when our surveyors reported that 90 percent of consumers said they would choose a V-8 over a six-cylinder engine even if the more powerful motor added a hundred-dollar premium to the price of the automobile. Many of the Chevrolet owners that we talked to said they would be very interested in a V-8 option, too. I didn't mean to do General Motors' research for them, but there it was. It was obvious to me that very soon Chevrolet had to answer our V-8 with one of its own.

We talked to dealers, too. We asked them what they thought of the V-8 and how difficult it would be to sell the Ford car if it only had a six. The dealers, in essence, said the same thing I had said to Crusoe: the V-8 *was* the Ford car. Without it, they did not think they could compete with Chevrolet. It was the reason why people bought Ford cars. We also asked the dealers how much more they thought they could get customers to

---

20 Hurley would go on to become the head of the Curtiss-Wright Corporation.

pay for the bigger engine. Once again, the figure that most of them came up with was one hundred dollars.

The results of Hurley's analysis were far better than I had hoped for, too. They showed that using the new manufacturing technology, we could produce a V-8 engine for only sixteen dollars more than a six-cylinder motor. I was thrilled! That meant that we could not only cover the added cost of the V-8 but actually make more money than we could selling cars equipped with a six—assuming we charged the hundred-dollar premium that most consumers said they were willing to pay. I now had everything I needed to prove my case for the V-8.

By the time my ninety days were up, I was ready. All of the data prepared by Hurley and my market-research team had been transcribed onto those same forty-by-sixty boards that had been the bane of my early days at the Ford Motor Company. I told Crusoe I was ready for him to make the presentation to Mr. Ford, Mr. Breech, and the other senior executives. The meeting was scheduled for April 1949.

The day before the meeting, Reith and I went to Crusoe's office to go over everything with him one more time so that he would be ready for any questions they might ask. But it turned out Crusoe had other ideas.

"Listen, it's your idea," he said, pointing to me. "As product planning manager, I think you should make the presentation."

I was too naïve to realize that Crusoe was trying to put some distance between himself and my proposal. He knew there would be some opposition to keeping the V-8, and Breech in particular had a reputation for being mean. He was known to just tear people apart. By sitting on the sidelines, Crusoe hoped to control the situation—but also hoped to let me bear the brunt of Breech's wrath if it came to that.

As enthusiastic as I was about making the case for the V-8, I began to worry that night as I thought about what would be at stake in tomorrow's meeting. I had never met any of these men in person, but their reputations loomed large over American business. I was confident that

I now had the facts I needed to support my arguments, but I realized they still might not welcome a young man like myself showing them the flaws in their thinking. Though the data supported my position, I knew I might still find myself on the street when all was said and done. I had a hard time falling asleep that night.

The meeting was held in Ford's boardroom—a round chamber dominated by a large, horseshoe-shaped table fashioned out of rich, blond wood. Seated around this table were the men who ran the legendary automaker. Henry Ford II sat at the center, opposite the opening. He was flanked by his brother, Benson, and Ernest Breech, along with Crusoe and other officers of the company. Their lieutenants sat on another circle of chairs that ringed the perimeter of the room. I recognized them all—they were some of the most powerful men in American business—but the only one I knew well was Robert McNamara. He was seated in one of the chairs behind Breech, but his presence there offered little reassurance.

I walked to the opening opposite Mr. Ford with as much confidence as I could muster. I had put on my funeral suit, figuring it might be appropriate for the occasion. The tension in the room was palpable. After all, these were the same men who had approved the plan to do away with the V-8 just a few months before, and they were not the sort to readily admit that they were wrong. I, on the other hand, was still a new hire, who still could not eat in the executive dining room. I understood their position, and I knew that they had made their decision based on what they thought was best for the Ford Motor Company. But I also knew that all the data I needed to prove them wrong was displayed on a series of boards mounted on easels behind me and in the thick binders I carried under my arm. I cleared my throat and began my presentation.

"For the past three months, I and my team have been talking to dealers and to customers, asking them what they think about the decision to do away with the V-8. The results of our research are here on these charts," I said, gesturing to the easels. "As you can clearly see, there is a strong preference for the V-8 engine, so strong, in fact, that ninety percent of consumers told us that they would be willing to pay up to one hundred dollars more for a car equipped with one than they would for the same automobile equipped with a six-cylinder motor."

That certainly got their attention. I then turned to the question of manufacturing costs.

"I know that many of you believe that the V-8 engine is simply too expensive for us to build," I said. "But by employing the latest manufacturing techniques, we can reduce the cost differential between a V-8 and a six to just sixteen dollars."

There were murmurs of surprise among the astonished executives.

When I was finished, Breech began peppering me with questions. It was immediately clear that he was running the meeting. Fortunately, a friend had advised me to expect a regular grilling from him, so I was ready for him. I had been told the best way to respond to his queries was to say, "Well, that's a good question, Mr. Breech. Here's what we found..." So that is exactly what I did. I would then open one of the books and read some direct quotes from dealers or customers that spoke to his concern. That seemed to work, though his relentless probing was exhausting.

As tough as he was on me, I liked Breech immediately. This was not a man who had risen to the top through nepotism or boardroom politics; this was a man who had ascended the corporate ladder by dint of his own talent and intelligence. I could tell that he was smart, and his questions were, too. They were some of the toughest and most challenging questions I had ever heard. They made me think—and the harder they made me think, the better my answers became. But Breech was not easily satisfied.

"How can you be so sure?" Breech kept asking me.

"Because, Mr. Breech, if you've got ninety percent of the people willing to pay a hundred dollars more for an engine that will only cost us sixteen dollars more to produce, then there is no reason to doubt," I said. "The facts speak for themselves."

It was the toughest meeting I had ever been in. I knew going in that those men were not simply going to take me at my word. But I never expected them to challenge my facts so vociferously. I later learned that the Finance team had previously made its own case for why it was too expensive to keep building the V-8, so Breech and the other executives were even more disinclined to accept my argument than I expected them to be. But I kept coming back to the data—to what our customers and dealers had said, to what our manufacturing experts had proved—and I could see that Breech and the others were beginning to wonder if they had made the right decision after all.

I also told them about my own experiences as a Ford owner. It was probably the first time in the history of the Ford Motor Company that an actual customer, albeit one disguised as a Ford product planner, had addressed the top management of the company! And I held nothing back. I spoke passionately and fearlessly about a subject that I'd had first-hand experience with since I was sixteen years old. My words were not filtered through layers of bureaucracy or twisted by the internal politics of the company. I kept hammering away at their objections and driving home my main point: that all the cost savings in the world are worthless if customers don't want to buy the product.

"The V-8 engine *is* the Ford car," I said over and over again. "It is also the *only* advantage we have over Chevrolet!"

Breech just stared at me. I stared back, waiting for his next question. But he was silent for what seemed like an eternity. It had been two hours since I began my presentation. To me, it felt like two years. I began to wonder if I had gone too far. Maybe I had not gone far enough. But I didn't know what else I could say to sway them. Mr. Ford and the other executives had turned to Breech, too, but he kept staring at me. Finally, Breech leaned back in his chair and raised his right hand.

"I vote that we keep the V-8 engine," he said.

Chapter Four

BREAKING IT DOWN

T hat one sentence made my career with the Ford Motor Company. Many of the executives in that room left stunned at what had just transpired—amazed that a young man who had only been with the company for a few months had just convinced the most powerful men in Dearborn to change their minds. But they were equally amazed by the avalanche of data that I had unleashed in support of my argument. In those days, too many decisions at Ford were still made by gut instinct and seat-of-the-pants thinking. I had marshaled the facts just as I had learned to do in Statistical Control, and I had used them to change the course of the Ford Motor Company forever. The 1952 Ford *would* have a V-8. And it was a lucky thing for Ford that it did.

While it is hard to say for sure what would have happened if Ford had killed the V-8, it doesn't take too much imagination to guess at the likely results. By early 1951, it would have been widely known that Ford was getting ready to replace its vaunted V-8 with a new overhead-valve six-cylinder motor for 1952. The automotive press would probably have speculated—incorrectly—that a new overhead-valve V-8 was also in the works and would follow sometime later. Auto writers would have been disappointed to learn the truth: the new Ford was not even designed to accommodate a larger engine. They still might have praised the power and efficiency of the new Ford six when it arrived in late 1951, but more than a few would have wondered aloud about what Ford was thinking.

Die-hard Ford fans would have been even more vocal and vociferous in their criticism of the company's decision to abandon the V-8. Many would have asked themselves the same question: "Why not just buy a Chevy?"

A marketing study prepared by my office estimated that the decision to kill the V-8 would have cost Ford approximately 300,000 car and truck sales annually. That amounted to more than 20 percent of the Ford brand's 1949–1950 volume. As it was, Ford's sales fell sharply in 1952 because of a short model year and strict government limits on civilian automobile production imposed as a result of the Korean conflict.[21]

Without the V-8, Ford would have fared much worse. At this point, Ford's management would have begun to recognize the blunder they had made in eliminating the V-8, but by then rectifying their error would have been a difficult and expensive proposition—requiring major engineering changes to the Ford car. To reduce both weight and costs, the original design for the '52 Ford had no structural provision for accommodating the larger engine. Even if it did, there would have been no V-8s to put in it. While the company would have continued to produce V-8s for its Lincoln and Mercury brands, the lines that produced motors for the Ford Division would already have been retooled and converted to six-cylinder production.

Imagine Ford's dismay and despair then when, in 1953, it was revealed that General Motors was readying a new V-8 engine for its 1955 Chevrolet![22] Apparently, GM had done some market research of its own and discovered the same preference for the bigger motor that my own surveys had revealed.[23] To counter this new threat, Ford would have

---

21 See Brinkley, pp.553–554, and Howley. "SIA Comparison Report: The New and the Old: 1952 Six vs. V8," reprinted in Terry Ehrich, *Special Interest Autos* and Richard A. Lentinello, *The Hemmings Motor News Book of Postwar Fords* (Bennington, Vermont: Hemmings Motor News, 2000), p. 32.

22 The automotive press was already speculating on the Chevrolet V-8 by early 1953; e.g., "Parade of 1953 Cars," *Popular Mechanics*, Vol. 99, No. 2 (February 1953), p. 106.

23 According to author Anthony Young, Chevrolet had begun work on an OHV V-8 around 1950, though that initial concept was abandoned in early 1952 in favor of a clean-sheet design developed under Chevrolet's new chief engineer, Edward N. Cole. See Anthony Young, *Classic Chevy Hot Ones: 1955–1957* (Ann Arbor, Mich.: Lowe & B. Hould Publishers, 2002), pp. 28–56.

been forced to launch a crash program to redesign its cars and trucks to accommodate a V-8. That would have been followed by extensive road testing under different climate conditions.

At the same time, Ford would have had to begin retooling the engine factories that it had just finished converting to six-cylinder production. This would have dramatically increased Ford's capital spending and undermined quality, because such unplanned changes are never easy. Crash retooling programs often lead to errors on the assembly line; the more quickly Ford reintroduced the V-8 engine, the greater the likelihood that the redesigned cars would have suffered the sort of production issues that marred the '49 Ford.

Sixty years later, we can only speculate about how long it would have taken for Ford to get redesigned V-8 cars and trucks into showrooms. While the Ford engineers who could have answered that question are no longer with us, I recently posed it to one of the company's top engineers of the 1970s. Former chief engineer Charlie Knighton told me that, based on his experience, making such extensive changes could have taken as long as thirty months.[24]

However long it took, Ford dealers would have struggled in the meantime as loyal customers, many of whom had been attracted to Ford in the first place because of its V-8, defected to Chevrolet. It probably would have taken several years for Ford to completely rectify its mistake. Recovering the sales momentum and market share lost during that time would have taken even longer. Ford probably would have survived (unlike some of the independents, such as Hudson and Kaiser, who were crippled by their lack of a V-8), but the Ford brand might well have sacrificed its number-two sales slot, much less any hope of unseating Chevrolet as the number-one brand in the country. Fortunately for the Ford family, the company's employees, and its dealers, we will never know.

---

24 Knighton called the idea of dropping the V-8 "crazy." He recalled racing his Ford V-8 against Chevrolets and "beating the hell out of them" as a young man. "The V-8 engine was the Ford car," he said, echoing my own words on the matter.

I recognize that some people might think Ford's leaders would have realized their mistake with the V-8 and taken action in time to avoid these problems. However, that assumption ignores two important facts: First, the executives running Ford at that time came from a GM culture where failure was not contemplated. They believed they knew how to engineer and build the best cars. Second, they believed that no special market research or focus groups were required to demonstrate that Ford only needed a six-cylinder engine. As far as they were concerned, that "fact" had already been proven by Chevrolet, which only offered a six-cylinder engine and, yet, was the best-selling car on the market. The rest of the company supported the decision because they admired and respected the leadership of these former GM executives. After all, Henry Ford II himself had hired them to make his company more like General Motors.

During the ninety days I spent building my case for the V-8, I had an opportunity to speak with many different people at all levels of the company. I found that most of them accepted the decision to eliminate the popular motor. Even the Whiz Kids had been convinced that killing the V-8 was the best thing for the bottom line. If I hadn't been there, I don't think anybody would have opposed it. Everybody thought it was a good idea, at least until I showed them why it wasn't.

Although none of us—myself included—realized it at the time, the history of the Ford Motor Company was forever altered as soon as Lewis Crusoe walked down the hall to tell Ernest Breech that a young man in Product Planning had just come into his office and told him that the plan they had put together was wrong. It is to both men's credit that they did not simply fire me on the spot. Breech and Crusoe were no dummies. They were among the most respected men in the automobile industry. In Dearborn, they walked on water. That they were willing to hear me out was amazing in itself; that they were willing to admit that they were wrong after listening to my presentation was the mark of true leadership.

I was thrilled that I had managed to persuade Ernest Breech and the other executives to keep the V-8. I was just a few months into my career at Ford, but I had already made my mark on the company. People knew who I was now, and they were beginning to see why there needed to be someone on the team who was looking out for the product—not just the bottom line. The decision to reverse course on the V-8 had proven the value of the Product Planning Department. Breech had validated that by his decision to reverse course based on my research. From now on, Ford would listen to its customers and its dealers before making any big product decisions. It was a major change in the way the company—and, indeed, the automobile industry—did business.

Other automakers heard about the Ford Motor Company's Product Planning Department and replicated it in their own organizations. But Ford was the first, and it maintained its lead for a long time. Former GM executive John DeLorean would later recall that after he became general manager of Chevrolet, angry Chevy dealers complained constantly about Ford's lead in product development, saying, "Why does Ford always get better products than we do?"[25]

As the Product Planning Department grew, I tried to find talented people to fill each new position. I didn't care much about where they went to school or how high their grade-point average was; I was looking for people who understood the customer and had a feel for the market. It was a gut-level thing, and I could usually tell who had it and who didn't pretty quickly in an interview.

I remember I got a call once from Mr. Ford himself, who said he had found a perfect addition for my department.

"Chase, I'm sending over a fellow to see you. He's got some of the most impressive references I've ever seen," Ford said. "I've never seen such recommendations from so many people—big people!"

Sure enough, this guy had impeccable credentials. He had a master's in economics from Harvard and a whole stack of letters of

---

25 DeLorean described these meetings in his own words in J. Patrick Wright's book, *On a Clear Day You Can See General Motors: John Z. DeLorean's Look Inside the Automotive Giant* (Chicago: Avon Books, 1979) pp. 129–131.

recommendation from influential figures in business and government—including one from Eisenhower! But something struck me as not quite right about the man. So after I had finished interviewing him, I went down to the personnel office and asked them to verify all of his references. It turned out they were all forgeries!

We ended up with about thirty people in Product Planning after I added a Competitive Analysis Department, a product of my second Christmas vacation at the company.

At the end of 1949, I went home to St. Louis for the holidays. General Motors had a factory there that I knew was producing the new 1950 Chevrolet, which was supposed to be getting a major face-lift. I decided to drive out to the plant and see what I could see. The parking lot there was full of the new Chevys! So I hired a local photographer and asked him to meet me there. We managed to get pictures of the new car from every angle, including the all-important grille and rear-end.

When I got back to Dearborn, I showed the photos to Lewis Crusoe. He was very impressed and sent them around to the other executives. People began to ask me if I could do it again, and that led to the formation of the Competitive Analysis Department—a group of guys that I would send out to places like GM's proving grounds in Milford, Michigan, to spy on the competition and take pictures of their new products.

><><

Of course, I didn't get to pick every employee myself.

One day, I was told that I would be getting a new addition to my team: William Clay Ford Sr.—Henry Ford II's brother and another grandson of old Henry Ford himself. I swallowed hard and promised to make him feel welcome on the team. We called him Clay and did our best to make him feel like one of the boys, but it didn't work out too well. Still, he and I remained friends and have played golf regularly through the years. We're pretty much the only guys left from those days. I liked Bill Ford Sr., and I remain a great admirer of his.

I also became a great admirer of Crusoe. He was a straight shooter with a great deal of talent and integrity, who never tried to sugarcoat the truth. He did quite the opposite: if he walked into the design studio and saw something he didn't like, Crusoe would shake his head and say, "Look, fellas, you can't nickel-plate a crowbar!"

He had some marvelous sayings. My favorite was the one he would use whenever we lost a battle with some other department. Crusoe would shake his head and sigh. "The Santa Fe Chief went through town sideways today." I loved that saying! I don't know where he got that from, but I loved it.

Over time, I also became friends with Breech. He was from Missouri, too, so that helped. He and I started playing golf together, and I discovered that—despite his dour demeanor at that first meeting—he was a very funny man who loved good jokes. I was very fond of him, and I always thought it was a shame that Henry Ford II didn't make him president of the company.

But I liked Mr. Ford, too. I often had to defend him to my friends because of his notoriety. He may have gotten in trouble because of his drinking and womanizing, which became fodder for the tabloids, but I will say this: he always showed up for work on time, and when he was at the office, he was always working hard to make his company successful. Mr. Ford did have one issue with me, and that was my golf skills. He had seen my name on the board at Grosse Pointe and Seminole, and he would tell his friends, "There's nobody who could play golf as good as Chase does and work as hard as he claims to!"

><>><

I thought that Breech's decision to keep the V-8 had settled the matter of the 1952 Ford, but it had not. The guys in Finance were pretty sore at me for showing them up in front of Breech, Mr. Ford, and the other executives, so they continued to throw up objections, claiming the car was still too expensive to build. I decided to settle the matter once and for all.

Crusoe had educated me about the importance of what he called "design cost." Design cost refers to the actual price of producing a given product, assuming the use of the best manufacturing and assembly processes currently available. Nobody had paid much attention to that at the Ford Motor Company, but I knew that it was an important piece of information to have if we wanted to understand how our products stacked up against those of our competitors.

The *actual* cost of producing a single car or truck can vary considerably, depending on the efficiency of the company's workers and factories, tooling amortization schedules, and other factors; the design cost represents the standardized best-case scenario for how much each car is *designed* to cost. Knowing it allows for "apples to apples" comparisons between products made in different factories or by different companies.

Up until then, Ford's Finance Department had only considered the actual production cost of the company's vehicles. But that factored in manufacturing inefficiencies, labor costs, and other expenses that had nothing to do with the actual design of the vehicle itself. I wanted to be able to show how much it would cost to build a Ford and a Chevrolet if each were built to the same standard in the same highly efficient factory. That way, we could arrive at the true cost differential between the two products. So I went to see Crusoe again.

"Mr. Crusoe, I want to answer the objections once and for all," I said. "Let's get a Chevy and a Ford and take them both apart and have the Manufacturing staff cost them out."

He agreed. So I ordered a brand-new Chevrolet and asked the factory to send me a Ford with the same features. I had both cars taken out to the Ford parts depot at Plymouth and Middlebelt Roads in Livonia, in the building where we were being housed while the new Ford Division headquarters was being built. There I had Roy Hurley's group disassemble the cars and analyze each of their components to figure out how much they actually cost. I had them mount each piece of each subassembly on large boards that could be wheeled around for presentation purposes. That way I could, for example, display the steering components from the

Chevrolet next to those from the Ford and explain the cost differences between the two systems. It took a couple of months for the men to finish their analysis, but I knew the exercise would be worthwhile.

The final tally proved my point. Once I had it, Crusoe asked the entire Product Planning Committee—including Henry Ford II—to meet us at the parts depot. One by one, I rolled the boards out and highlighted the cost differences between the two cars.

"Gentlemen, the cost of our Ford car, even with the V-8, is actually twenty dollars *less* than the cost of the Chevrolet," I said. "The problem, therefore, lies with manufacturing, not with design or engineering or the V-8!"

That settled the matter. This time, there was no room for doubt. The Finance people had always complained that Ford's designers and engineers had created vehicles that were too expensive relative to the competition. I demonstrated that this was simply not the case. The designs were not too costly; Ford was just less efficient at producing cars than its rivals. If Ford wanted to close the cost gap with Chevrolet, it needed to do so on the factory floor—not on the drafting table.

There were no more objections from Finance about the '52 Ford, but there continued to be considerable friction between the Finance staff and my own Product Planning office. They continued to insist that the things we wanted—better quality and improved features—were just too expensive.

We soon locked horns over the automatic transmission, which became available as an option on Ford cars in 1951. Chevrolet had introduced their own optional automatic a year earlier, and it was a big hit with consumers.[26] I had been arguing that we needed to offer an automatic almost as long as I had been fighting for the V-8, and I encountered almost as much resistance from Finance. They particularly did not like the new transmission factory we had to build in Cincinnati.[27] It was

26 The Chevrolet Powerglide transmission was optional beginning with the 1950 model year.
27 The Cincinnati Automatic Transmission Factory opened in 1950. It produced the first Ford-O-Matic and Merc-O-Matic three-speed automatic transmissions based on a design licensed from Borg Warner. Demand was so great that a second automatic-transmission plant was opened in Livonia, Michigan, in 1954.

a real knock-down, drag-out fight, but I won that battle, too. One of the reasons that I fought so hard for the automatic transmission was because I remembered what a tough time I'd had learning to drive a manual transmission when I was sixteen. I never forgot how hard it was for me to master that damn clutch, and I figured many Ford customers would appreciate not having to struggle with one.

Despite these conflicts, I had great respect for the top Finance guys—Ed Lundy and Arjay Miller. I never felt any of our disagreements rose to the level of animosity or unpleasantness. We all had jobs to do. Finance played a very important role at Ford. As frustrating our arguments could be, I came to value them. They forced my team and me to do our homework, to stress test our assumptions, and to really think through our product strategy. Product Planning's job was to marshal the facts; we had to make sure that we always had the data required to support our point of view. Whenever my staff complained about Finance's resistance, I would remind them that they were just doing their job and making sure we did ours.

"They're making us better product planners," I would tell my team.

The 1952 Ford finally arrived in showrooms in February of that year, sporting an all-new body shell and styling.[28] Although the new "Mileage Maker Six" was offered as the standard engine, buyers could—for a just a little bit more money—opt for the more powerful "Strato-Star V-8." Though essentially the same as the old flathead motor, it had been revamped to produce even more horsepower and maintain its superiority over the six-cylinder engine.[29] The overwhelming majority of customers chose the V-8, just as I knew they would. Ford did not break out production figures by engine type in this era, but industry estimates

---

28 The styling was the work of Joe Oros of George Walker Associates, then a design consultant for the Ford Motor Company.
29 The improved V-8 offered 110 horses to the six-cylinder's 101.

suggest that fewer than 50,000 '52 Fords were sold with the six-cylinder engine—just over 7 percent of the total produced.[30]

Ford continued producing the old L-head V-8 through 1953 in the United States (and through 1954 in Canada). After that, it was replaced by an all-new "Y-block" overhead valve V-8 that was considerably more powerful than the flathead engine. Derivatives of this motor would continue to power Ford cars and trucks through 1962, when it was replaced by an even more powerful V-8.

Most historians have assumed that the upgraded flathead V-8 Ford offered in 1952 and 1953 was just a stopgap. They have speculated that production restrictions imposed as a result of the Korean War were the only reason why the automaker waited until 1954 to put the new V-8 in a Ford.[31] But the reality was that Ford's engineers were not even working on a new overhead-valve V-8 until we pushed them.

Charles Patterson, then the head of Ford's Engine Division, had just retooled the engine plant at the Rouge Complex to make yet another improved version of the flathead motor. I argued that since Oldsmobile had just introduced a new overhead-valve V-8, we were going to have to build one, too, in order to maintain our leadership position in the entry-level V-8 market. Patterson asked me to meet him over at the factory.

"Look!" he shouted over the din of production. "I have to tear all this apart! All this money, wasted!"

But I knew we had to have a modern V-8, not just an improved version of the old engine, and I pushed it through. Patterson never forgave me as long as I was at the company, but the new V-8 was a huge success. By 1955, Lewis Crusoe was publicly predicting that Ford would phase out six-cylinder motors entirely by 1960 because of lack of demand from the car-buying public!

---

30 John Gunnell, ed. *Standard Catalog of American Cars 1946–1975*. Rev. 4th ed. (Iola, Wis.: Krause Publications, 2002), pp. 390–391.

31 Lincolns got the new V-8 in 1952.

Chapter Five

THE APPLE IN THE WINDOW

A rmed with its new V-8 engine, Ford almost managed to catch up with Chevrolet in 1954. The sales tallies were so close and there were so many allegations of number fudging on both sides that it would take until the following year for independent analysts to conclude that Chevy was still number one. But only just.[32] What was clear to everyone, including the guys at General Motors, was that Ford was back. We were so close to victory, we could taste it. Of course, our rivals at GM were not resting, so we could not either. It was no secret that Chevrolet was working on something big—a true American sports car. It would be called the *Corvette*, and those of us in Product Planning at Ford knew we needed something big to counter this new threat.

Rakish, two-seat sports cars had long been popular in Europe. American GIs discovered them there after the war and started bringing home British MGs and Italian Alfa Romeos. In 1951, Nash Motors introduced the Nash-Healey, but like the imports, it was too expensive for most consumers.[33] Legendary GM designer Harley Earl had always been a fan of sports cars, and he persuaded his bosses that there was a real opportunity for a more moderately priced American roadster to

---

32 John K. Teahen Jr., "Chevy and Ford Have Waged a Sales Battle for a Century," *Automotive News*, Oct. 31, 2011.

33 The Nash-Healey was developed with help from Britain's Donald Healey and Italy's Pininfarina.

make a big splash in the market. Earl and his team began work on their supposedly top-secret "Project Opel" in late 1951.

But we were onto them.

Early in 1952, a former GM colleague showed sketches of the car that would become the Corvette to Ford's chief stylist, Frank Hershey. Hershey was impressed, and he and several other Ford designers—Bill Boyer, Damon Woods, John "Dick" Samsen, and Allan Kornmiller— began work on their own sports car using Hershey's new Jaguar XK-120 as inspiration.[34] This was strictly an off-the-books effort. Engineering had not authorized it. That was a major breach of protocol. In those days, Styling had to have a work order from Engineering before they could even start sharpening their pencils.

When Ford's chief engineer, Earle MacPherson, found out about the unauthorized sports car, he almost killed the project. But I talked him out of it. I was one of the few people outside of Styling who knew about the top-secret sports car project, and I approved of it wholeheartedly. We needed cars like this to capture the public's imagination and give them a reason to come to our showrooms. MacPherson was a dour man, who seemed to be perpetually scowling. His discovery of the secret sports car project did little to soften those qualities. But MacPherson was also calm and level-headed, and I was sure I could make him see the value of the car Hershey and his team were working on.

"You know, Mac, we need something like this to pep up the brand and draw attention to the rest of the Ford cars," I told him. "We need to have something to answer what Chevrolet is doing."

Reluctantly, MacPherson agreed.

Hershey himself would later recount this story in an interview with Richard Langworth for his book, *The Thunderbird Story: Personal Luxury.* "My boss, E.S. MacPherson...came in and found out (about the model)," Hershey said. "He was hopping mad—not because we'd started the project but because we hadn't told him anything about it. Chase

---

34   Michael Lamm and Dave Holls, *Century of Automotive Style: 100 Years of American Car Design* (Stockton, Calif.: Lamm-Morada Publishing Co. Inc., 1997), p. 143.

Morsey came to bat for us. He thought it was a great idea. He was the best of the 'Whiz Kids.'"[35]

>=×=<

Hershey and his team were allowed to continue work on their sports car, but the project still stalled in late 1952. However, it was revived in earnest once the Corvette made its public debut at the New York Motorama in January 1953. When Lewis Crusoe saw that stunning roadster sparkling in the camera flashes, he wanted to know why Ford didn't have a sports car of its own in the pipeline. Within days, Hershey's project was formally approved by the Product Planning Committee.

As a car guy, I was thrilled that the top brass had given the green light to the project, but I was less enthusiastic about the car itself now that I'd had some time to think about it. I still believed that we needed to respond to the Corvette, but I didn't think we needed to imitate it. The Corvette was patterned after a race car. It wouldn't have roll-up windows or even door handles. I thought that would limit its appeal. Only die-hard motoring enthusiasts would be willing to put up with such austerity.

Many of my colleagues at Ford thought our car should be a real sports car, too—one aimed at the crash helmet and goggles set. Our car wasn't even going to have windows, let alone an automatic transmission. The more I thought about it, the more concerned I became about the market for this car. Like the Corvette, it would turn heads, but I doubted we would sell enough of them to make a real impact. Contemporary sports cars were too crude in both features and finish.

I thought we could do better by offering a sporty car that still featured all the modern amenities to which American motorists were now accustomed. I wanted a car that was more refined, one with real windows, an elegant interior, and a full array of upscale options from power steering to power brakes. I had an image in my mind of what our car could be: I pictured a beautiful blonde cruising effortlessly up the Pacific

---

35 Of course, as I have already explained, I was not "officially" one of the original Whiz Kids.

Coast Highway in California with the top down. That was a car that would sell! I began referring to it as a "personal car," and I started lobbying hard for us to go in this direction.

Hershey acknowledged my role in developing this concept:

I was with Morsey alone in the studio around that time, discussing what to call it...During the discussion, he went over several ideas. He did not think 'sports car' would fill the bill. He wanted a car that would be acceptable to a banker, for instance, who could drive up to his bank without feeling self-conscious, or a searcher for lost youth. Then Chase brightened up and said, 'I know what we'll call it—a personal car.' And that was it. Crusoe has received a lot of credit for things he didn't do. It was Morsey who wanted—along with us—to make the car as luxurious as possible.[36]

Bill Boyer, one of the chief designers of the Thunderbird, also talked about my role in coming up with the "personal car" concept in his book, *Thunderbird: An Odyssey in Automotive Design*: "Chase had defined the Thunderbird as a personal car with all the options and amenities that the word 'personal' implies."[37]

My idea for the Ford Sports Car, as it was then known, ran into considerable resistance. Some of the designers and engineers objected. They still wanted a real Ford racer. The Finance Department also had issues with my proposal, arguing that luxury amenities were not important to sports car customers. Of course, they also thought it would be too expensive to build. This time, I surprised them by admitting that the car was unlikely to make money for Ford in its own right. But that didn't mean it wouldn't boost Ford's profits.

"This car will be the apple in the window," I told the Finance people. "True, we won't make any money on it, but we're going to make a lot of money off the other Ford cars it sells for us!"

---

36 Richard Langworth, *The Thunderbird Story: Personal Luxury* (Osceola, Wis.: Motorbooks International, 1980), p. 28.

37 William P. Boyer, *Thunderbird: An Odyssey in Automotive Design* (Dallas: Taylor Publishing Company, 1986), p. 42.

They had never considered anything like this before, but once I laid it out for them, they could see the merit of this strategy. I persuaded the other executives that this was the best way to answer Chevrolet.

>◁◁▷◁

As always, the role of the Product Planning Department in the Thunderbird project was to be the voice of the customer. We never designed a car, like Styling did, or worked out the schematics, like Engineering, but we were involved in all of these things. Our job was to furnish ideas of how the public might react to something. We weren't the decision makers, but we were idea creators.

"Under Morsey's influence, (Ford) engineered room for accessories like power brakes, steering, windows, and seats," noted Thunderbird historian Langworth.[38]

I know that questions about who designed which part of the Thunderbird are the subjects of many bitter arguments by enthusiasts and historians. All I can say for sure is that it wasn't me. Crusoe had a real feel for styling, and he and I made many trips to the design studio to check on the progress of the clay model, but we only offered feedback and suggestions. I may have come up with the idea for what the Thunderbird should be, but I did not come up with its iconic styling—though I did have some say in what the finished product looked like. For example, I suggested to George Walker, Ford's styling consultant on the Thunderbird, that the designers should base the car's detachable hardtop on the roof of the soon-to-be-unveiled Continental Mark II. They did just that, with beautiful results—though William Clay Ford was not as thrilled about it as the rest of us. He had been named general manager of the newly formed Continental Division and was a little peeved by the swipe.

"The idea for the blind quarter came when Chase Morsey came to the Continental Division for a sneak look. We were months ahead of

---

38 Langworth, p. 29.

the T-Bird in clay, and he 'borrowed' our roof line for a car that was to precede the Mark II by a year," Ford is quoted as saying in Boyer's book.[39]

I still feel a little guilty about borrowing one of the Mark II's major design cues, and I now apologize to Clay for any hurt feelings it may have caused. But the hardtop was gorgeous!

I also lobbied hard for a unique color palette. I thought the Thunderbird deserved color options that were all its own. I was thrilled when Bob Maguire, Ford's executive stylist, showed us some of the new colors he and his team had picked out that would be exclusive to the T-Bird. The turquoise, officially known as "Thunderbird Blue," was one of the prettiest things I ever saw!

Other writers have already noted the role I played in thwarting a late attempt by Walker to promote an alternative design by his lieutenant, Joe Oros.[40] That was not uncommon in this period; Walker's contract with Ford specifically authorized him to propose alternatives to the in-house designs.[41] Hershey and Oros had originally created the second car to beef up their presentation to the Product Planning Committee as part of the effort to win approval for a Ford sports car. But Walker began a quiet campaign to convince Crusoe to adopt Oros's version instead of the one designed by Hershey and his team. I preferred the in-house design and convinced Crusoe to stick with it. I stood behind the Hershey version because I thought it was just a better-looking car.[42]

The styling of the Ford sports car was approved in mid-1953, but it was still not clear how or where the car would be built. Some at Ford wanted to follow Chevrolet's example and build the body out of fiberglass. That would eliminate the need for the costly tooling required for a steel body. But Henry Grebe, the chief body engineer, insisted that the Ford sports car be built of metal. Finance was reluctant to authorize the

39 Boyer, p. 33.

40 Jim and Cheryl Farrell, *Ford Design Department: Concept & Showcars 1932–1961* (Hong Kong: World Print Ltd., 1999), p. 172.

41 David R. Crippen, "The Reminiscences of George W. Walker," April 1985, Automotive Design Oral History Project Accession 1673, Benson Ford Research Center.

42 Oros later denied doing a second version of the Thunderbird, but he did.

tooling expenditure for a low-volume vehicle such as this, arguing that Ford would never recoup its investment. And Manufacturing was not happy about disrupting production of the regular 1955 to squeeze in a specialty car.

I came up with a solution.

I called up the Budd Company, which had long produced body stampings for Ford, and asked about the possibility of using temporary tooling to produce the sports car. Temporary tooling—which is used by automakers for preproduction prototypes—is much cheaper to produce but degrades much more quickly than regular tooling. Using it would limit the number of cars we could produce before the tooling wore out, but it would greatly reduce Ford's initial investment in the new vehicle. The guys from Budd agreed that my plan could work. For once, so did Ford's Finance staff.[43]

To solve the production issue, the frame would be built by the A.O. Smith Corporation. To save even more money, the final design borrowed various pieces from the standard 1955 Ford—a move I was certain would also enhance the image of the entire Ford lineup. Everybody was happy, and the new car—now called the Thunderbird—was approved for production in September 1953.

><><

A full-size mock-up of the Thunderbird stole the show when it was unveiled at the annual Detroit Auto Show in February 1954. The car itself finally went on sale on October 22, 1954, as a 1955 model.

It was the most ambitiously priced product the Ford Division had ever offered. The base price was originally announced as $2,695, but that was raised to $2,944 in 1955.[44] That made it more than 25 percent more than a regular V-8 Ford convertible. The standard equipment included

43 Before World War II, Ford had used outside companies such as Budd and Briggs to make bodies for some low-volume production models, but had moved away from that practice after the war.

44 The Thunderbird's advertised price increased at least once, possibly twice, during the '55 model year—though many modern sources simply list it as $2,944, e.g., see John Gunnell, ed., *T-Bird: 40 Years of Thunder* (Krause Publications, 1995), p. 12.

windup windows, a four-way power bench seat, a tachometer, and a detachable fiberglass hardtop. A convertible soft-top was available as an option. Unlike the Corvette, the Thunderbird had a V-8 engine. A three-speed manual transmission was standard, although many buyers opted for the optional Ford-O-Matic. Just as I had intended, a host of other options were available, including power steering, brakes, windows, and even a power radio antenna. A full load of accessories added over $1,000 to the tab, putting the price into Lincoln, Cadillac, and even Jaguar territory. But I never thought about it in those terms; I was just thrilled with the prestige this car brought to the Ford brand.

The Thunderbird made news around the world and even won the respect of European critics—rare for any American car, then or now.[45] The automotive press had mixed feelings about the Thunderbird, praising its straight-line performance, but expressing some reservations about its relatively soft suspension.[46] That was by design. The T-Bird did not handle like a real sports car, but it offered a much more comfortable ride.

None of that criticism mattered though, because the public was smitten. The Thunderbird occupied a unique niche: It was expensive but not unattainable. And while it was sporty enough and fast enough to win the affection of street racers, it had the refinement and luxury to satisfy mature buyers, who would have considered a hard-core sports car, like the Austin-Healey 100, a little too raw. The Thunderbird was an immensely desirable car, one of those rare products that appealed equally to men and women, young and old, and celebrities and the common man alike. Only a few of the two-seater's many admirers would ever own one, but nearly everyone wanted to. First-year production totaled only 16,155 units. We could have sold a lot more, but that was all the temporary tooling would permit. The fact that demand so greatly exceeded the supply only enhanced the Thunderbird's mystique.

45 For example, see "The Autocar Road Tests No. 1588: Ford Thunderbird," *The Autocar*, Feb. 10, 1956, pp. 154–157.

46 See "Testing Ford's 'Personal' Car: The T-Bird Shows Its Claws," *Road & Track*, Vol. 6, No. 7 (March 1955) or "The Thunderbird," *Car Life*, Vol. 2, No. 5 (September 1955).

The Thunderbird drew customers to our dealerships in droves. People stood in line for hours just to get a look at it. Some of them bought T-Birds, but more of them bought less exotic Ford cars. Just as I knew it would, the Thunderbird spurred a big increase in sales for all Ford products. Our passenger car sales were up 24 percent for the 1955 model year.

✦✦✦

In December 1954, I wrote a report that outlined our plan for the Thunderbird and its continuing role in Ford's product strategy:

"General Motors can and is making product changes much more rapidly than in the past. In light of these developments, the importance of developing maximum product flexibility in our product plans has become increasingly apparent," I wrote. "The Thunderbird...is a permanent part of the Ford car line and will be planned as a personal car, not a sports car...Consideration will be given to the introduction of new Thunderbird models at a time different than that of regular cars, possibly in March to stimulate showroom traffic. The Thunderbird line should be planned to sell [for] $2,500–$2,700 list price, with options and accessories in the $4,000 delivered price range...Thunderbird model changes should not follow the regular passenger car pattern. Interim programs (when the body shell is not changed) should place special emphasis on mechanical and performance improvements and innovations such as fuel-injection systems, gas turbine engines, and independent rear suspensions. The normal type of appearance changes associated with interim year models for passenger cars are not adequate of themselves to stimulate Thunderbird customers to buy a new model. The incorporation of a retractable hardtop in future Thunderbird programs should be considered."[47]

Not all of these forward-looking ideas were actually adopted, but the two-seat Thunderbird remained in production through December 1957, undergoing various minor changes along the way. Revisions for 1956 included more powerful engines, a new hardtop with round "portholes"

---

47 As quoted in Langworth, pp. 33–34.

for better rear visibility, and a standard external spare tire—popularly known as the "Continental kit"—to improve cargo space. Midway through the year, Thunderbirds could also be ordered with Ford's much-publicized "Lifeguard" safety features, which included a padded dash and seat belts.[48] The Continental kit was eliminated in 1957, but the Thunderbird's tail was extended and restyled to incorporate small fins, like those on the standard '57 Fords. The car was lowered, thanks to smaller wheels, and more powerful engines were offered, which gave the Thunderbird even more credibility with performance enthusiasts.

We continued to sell every car we could build, with high transaction prices and outstanding resale values. I don't think the original Thunderbird ever made a dime, but it continued to draw customers into our showrooms and elevated Ford's image to an entirely new level. It was a major turning point in Ford's history. Here was where we really diverged from Chevrolet. Up until then, we had been following Chevy in almost everything it did. Now we were thinking for ourselves. We became leaders in our own right with the Thunderbird.

In early 1958, the two-seater was replaced by a low-slung, but significantly larger, four-seat Thunderbird, available either as a hardtop coupe or a convertible. Conceived as a styling exercise in late 1954, the four-seat concept was embraced by Robert McNamara, who had succeeded Lewis Crusoe as Ford Division general manager in early 1955.[49] I sold him on the idea. McNamara understood the brand-building value of the T-Bird, but he was also worried about its poor financial performance. The four-seater offered a better balance of prestige and profit, because it would appeal to a lot more customers. I told McNamara that it would allow us to double or even triple our volume, and it did. By 1960, the "Square Bird" was outselling upmarket cars, such as the Oldsmobile Ninety-Eight, and earning a very healthy profit for Ford.

---

48 This was a pet project of McNamara's, and it made the Ford Motor Company the safety leader, at least among domestic automakers.

49 Crusoe had been promoted to group vice president in charge of all of Ford's car and truck divisions.

The Thunderbird was so successful that it even saved the Corvette. It turned out that Chevrolet was about to pull the plug on its poor-selling sports car when the T-Bird made its debut in 1954. The guys at General Motors knew that if they followed through with their plan to kill the Corvette after that, it would be viewed as a concession of defeat.[50] So GM kept the Corvette in production long enough for it to become a credible high-performance car. The Corvette remained harder edged and sportier than the Thunderbird, but Chevrolet gradually introduced many of the same luxury features that Ford's Finance staff had so strenuously opposed, from power steering to power brakes. By 1961 the success of the four-seat Thunderbird even prompted GM to consider a four-passenger Corvette, although it never reached production.[51]

The Thunderbird marked the beginning of an exciting new era for Ford cars and trucks. Instead of chasing Chevrolet's tail, we pulled ahead of the competition in a way that we had not managed to do since Ford launched the flathead V-8 back in 1932. And we didn't stop there. Over the next two decades, the Thunderbird would be followed by a long line of innovative, category-defining Ford products, including the hugely popular Mustang. While Chevrolet still often held the lead in sales, thanks in large part to its stronger dealer network, it was now Ford's products that Chevy and the rest of the industry scrambled to copy.

The Ford cars and trucks built during this era were not necessarily the fastest or the most sophisticated or even the best-looking vehicles on the road. But they were often the best conceived. Because of the work of the Product Planning Office, they were developed with an astute understanding of what the car-buying public wanted and needed. With the Thunderbird, we came into our own as a third partner with Styling and Engineering.

---

50 Corvette chief engineer Zora Arkus-Duntov later admitted this. See Richard M. Langworth and the Auto Editors of Consumer Guide, *The Complete Book of Corvette* (New York: Beekman House, 1987), p. 45.

51 Michael Lamm, "Chevrolet's 'Almost' 4-Place Vette," *Special Interest Autos*, No. 60 (December 1980), pp. 20–21.

In the early 1960s, after I became marketing manager for the Ford Division, I would often run into Semon "Bunkie" Knudsen, Chevrolet's general manager, in the locker room of the Bloomfield Hills Country Club.

"Goddamn you!" he would complain good-naturedly. "Why do you keep making me work so hard?!"

Crusoe sometimes referred to the Thunderbird as "Chase's car." I was proud of that, but I was always clear that I neither designed nor styled this most iconic of American automobiles. I thought that Frank Hershey, who actually led the Thunderbird team, summed it up best when he told the writer Dennis Adler that I had defined the personal luxury concept and sold the idea to senior management.[52] Product Planning shepherded the Thunderbird through a difficult development process, and I championed the project at every stage. Although the Thunderbird would still have existed without me, it could easily have become a very different and much less successful product.

I never thought of the Thunderbird as my car, but I did think we were onto something with my idea of "an apple in the window." I came to believe that we should always strive to have a car like the Thunderbird at the head of our product lineup.

Apparently, other automakers agreed. Today, such cars are referred to as "halo vehicles" because of the aura that envelops the entire brand because of them. General Motors still has the Chevrolet Corvette. Chrysler has the SRT Viper. And Ford has the Shelby Mustang. Even the foreign automakers have followed suit with cars such as the BMW M3, the Mercedes-Benz SLS AMG, and the Nissan GT-R.

These are part of the legacy of the Thunderbird—a legacy that I am proud to have had a hand in forging. But the Thunderbird did more than move metal for the Ford Motor Company. The car made people

---

52 Dennis Adler, "Thirty Years of Flight," *Car Collector and Car Classics*, September 1985, and his later book, *Fifties Flashback: The American Car* (Osceola, Wis.: Motorbooks International, 1996), pp. 119–123.

smile. And that legacy has also endured. Thunderbirds remain one of the most collectible cars ever made, and I continue to hear from owners and enthusiasts who are eager to share just how much the T-Bird means to them. As John M. Smith, then president of the Classic Thunderbird Club International, said when I was elected to the Thunderbird Hall of Fame:

I believe no other domestically produced, modern day automobile has generated [more] excitement and loyalty than the classic Thunderbird. The styling of this car has transcended time...it is just as appealing and popular today as it was when it [rolled off] the factory assembly line. I am often reminded of the level of public appeal this car has every time I drive my '57 Thunderbird on the freeway because I always receive a thumbs-up or a honk of the horn from a passing admirer. The most common [word] I hear when somewhat walks up to my T-Bird at the local cruise night and lays eyes on it for the first time is "Wow!" That is exactly what the classic Thunderbird was over years ago and what it still is today.

Chapter Six

THE CAR THAT
BEAT CHEVY

W e did not rest on our laurels in the Product Planning Department. Our mission was to beat Chevrolet, and we were right on their tail. But we knew that the only way to pass them was by continuing to design and build the sort of cars and trucks that our customers wanted to buy. That meant understanding the consumer.

During my time as head of Product Planning at Ford, I was always keeping a sharp eye out for consumer trends and my mind was always working to come up with ideas for new products or ways of improving our existing vehicles. I carried a Dictaphone in my car so that I could record my thoughts and observations as I drove to and from work each day. I guess it was my creative nature. I was always studying the other cars on the road and getting ideas. If a feature of a passing car caught my eye, I would grab the microphone and make a note of it. I would drop these recordings off with my secretary, Ruth, when I came to work each day so that she could transcribe them. My staff would always kid her about this.

"How much work did Chase leave for you today?" they would ask with a grin.

In those days, we flew by the seat of our pants and navigated by gut instinct. Of course, we used the conventional forms of business analysis. We looked at price comparisons and compared our products with the competition, feature by feature. We studied sales reports and tried to identify trends. But my foremost concern was not with this sort of statistical analysis but with our dealers and customers. I wanted to understand their wants and needs so that I could figure out the factors that would make them choose a Ford over a Chevy.[53]

The prevailing belief in the automobile industry was that non-luxury customers were primarily motivated by price. Most analysts in Detroit believed that the main thing consumers who purchased Fords and Chevrolets wanted was the cheapest car possible. I knew intuitively that this simply wasn't true. Ford customers valued style, performance, and features and were willing to pay more for a better product. I had already proven that with my research on the V-8, but I continued to struggle against the prevailing mind-set.

While entry-level buyers were certainly concerned about the price of the automobile, few of them wanted to be perceived as cheap. I understood that for many people, a new Ford was every bit as aspirational as a Cadillac. There's just something about a new car—even the smell is exhilarating. My aim was to give them the excitement that they craved. My goal was to make Ford's products something worth dreaming about. I wanted our customers to drive off the lot with cars and trucks that they could be proud of owning and showing off to their family, friends, and neighbors.

That was why I continued to fight to add the latest features to our Ford cars. I always believed that Ford buyers wanted these options every bit as much as Lincoln buyers, and I did not think we should deny them, as long as they were willing to pay for them. To my mind, it just made good business sense to offer our customers a solid, reasonably priced base model and then offer a menu of optional features that would allow them to drive off with as much of a car as they could afford. Whatever Lincoln had, I wanted Ford to offer as well. Lincolns would always differentiate themselves with styling and the exclusivity of the brand itself.

This approach is fairly common today, but I had to fight for it back in the 1950s. Predictably, much of the resistance came from the Finance staff, which continued to argue that many of these innovations—features

---

53 The Chrysler Corporation was the number-three automaker in the United States in those days, but we never gave them much thought. Our focus was always on General Motors.

such as power steering and air conditioning—were just too expensive to put in the regular Ford car. As I mentioned, one of our first battles was over automatic transmissions, but that was not the only one. During the development of the '54 Ford, I lobbied hard not only for the V-8 but also for optional "Master-Guide" power steering, "Swift Sure" power brakes, "Power-Lift" electric windows and even a four-way power seat. These prestige features had been introduced on Lincolns only a year earlier.

Once again, my thinking proved correct: Chevrolet made all of these options available on its high-series models at almost the same time. If we had not had these features, our dealers would have been at a distinct disadvantage. With them, our dealers were thrilled. The availability of financing—particularly once Korean War-era restrictions on consumer credit were lifted in 1952—made up selling easy, boosting dealer profits and Ford's own bottom line.[54] The Ford-O-Matic transmission was fairly expensive, adding $184 to the price of a car in 1954. But it only added eight dollars a month to the typical twenty-four-month car loan.

The only feature that I failed to get added to the '54 Ford's options list was air conditioning. I fought hard for it, too, because I remembered how miserable I would get during the summertime in St. Louis. I kept pushing Engineering to develop a system for the Ford car. Bill Burnett, who was in charge of passenger car engineering at the time, told me they had prototypes running out on our test track in Yuma, Arizona, but they kept overheating. But I kept pushing him.

"Jeez, Bill, everybody else has it," I'd chide him. "Why can't we have air conditioning that works?"

Burnett insisted that it was not for lack of trying. He and his team were working on a better system than the big trunk-mounted units or weak below-dash air conditioners that were the norm in those days. Ford's engineers wanted to mount the air conditioner under the hood and integrate it with the heater to allow greater climate-control flexibility in all

---

54 Wartime "Measure W" required a down payment of 33 percent on new car purchases and limited financing terms to no more than eighteen months. The Federal Reserve rescinded the controversial measure in May 1952. See "State of Business: Step This Way, Please!" *Time*, Vol. 59, No. 20 (May 19, 1952), p. 99.

types of weather. Ultimately, they succeeded in doing just that. Ford's "SelectAire" system arrived in early 1955. Ford finally had air conditioning, albeit months after Chevrolet. It was an expensive option at $435, and there were few takers initially.[55] But it caught on as the price dropped.

Other than features, the big thing that separated Fords from their more upmarket competitors in the mid-1950s was sheer size. The 1955 Fords were hardly small, but contemporary mid-priced cars rode longer wheelbases, giving them distinctive proportions and promising more interior room and smoother ride—at least, in theory. Some of GM's mid-priced brands offered a choice of wheelbases, but this was rare in the low-priced segment. I figured that if we gave customers the option of a longer wheelbase on our high-series Fairlane models, it would give us a leg up on Chevrolet and help us compete in a more profitable arena.

Offering two wheelbases would involve both design and tooling changes, but I sold Engineering and Styling on the idea. With a few exceptions, most people in both departments got the spirit of what I was trying to do and supported the idea. I pitched the idea to Robert McNamara himself in early 1955.

McNamara and I were never close. Though we had served together during the war, we did not socialize outside of work. But we maintained a cordial working relationship. We would talk about cars and the things we wanted to do. He was tough on me but always very fair.[56] McNamara and I were usually the first ones in the office each morning, so I decided to approach him early, before anyone else arrived. I was ready for a fight.

"Bob, I have an idea of how we can get one up on Chevrolet: a longer wheelbase for our Fairlane series," I told him. "I think we can do it with some interchangeability in tooling."

---

55 According to one estimate, only 22,575 Ford cars—including some 1956 models—were built with SelectAire during the 1955 calendar year. See Gunnell, p. 395.

56 I feel that it is important to state that I never agreed with McNamara's handling of the Vietnam War. I thought it was disastrous.

McNamara smiled.

"Chase, I don't care how many wheelbases you've got," he said. "As long as you bring it in within some kind of reasonable tooling budget, go for it."

I almost fell out of my chair! I had expected him to object, and I had thought of all sorts of arguments that I would use to chip away at his objections and win him over to my way of thinking. McNamara was very strict about budgets and usually frowned at any suggestion that might force a recalculation.

Fortunately, that was not necessary in this case. Engineering worked out a way to extend the wheelbase of the Fairlane from 116 inches to 118 inches without investing in completely new tooling. That made the addition of a longer wheelbase version a lot less costly than it would otherwise have been. Once McNamara saw Styling's design for the car, he gave it his enthusiastic approval for the 1957 model year.

><><

Although I always coordinated my activities with my boss, Jack Reith, I had less and less contact with him as time went by. Reith trusted me and allowed me to work directly with Crusoe. When Reith was sent overseas to take charge of Ford of France in the fall of 1952, I took his place as manager of Product and Programming. Now my responsibilities were not limited to deciding which cars and trucks Ford should build; I was also responsible for figuring out how many and where. Making sure the Ford Division was making the best use of its many factories was a delicate balancing act that drew heavily on my experience at Air Materiel Command during the war. I also was responsible for managing the construction and location of new plants and parts depots.

All of this kept me quite busy. I was in the office by seven each morning and often did not get home until after nine in the evening. It was a stressful job. When I spent money for the Ford Motor Company, it was often in the hundreds of millions of dollars. That was a lot of responsibility to have resting on my still-young shoulders!

I relaxed the same way I always had—by playing golf. Because of the high-pressure environment we worked in at Product Planning, I was very conscious of the need to keep up morale. To that end, I started an annual tradition called "Chase Morsey Day." Each year, I would invite the entire staff to a buffet lunch and an afternoon of golf and other games at my country club, followed by a celebratory dinner. I would hand out prizes to the best golfer, to the man who had shown the most improvement since the previous year, and so on. Everyone enjoyed himself thoroughly and returned to the office in high spirits.

In 1955, golf legend Chris Dunphy invited me to join the prestigious Seminole Golf Club in North Palm Beach, Florida. Henry Ford II was also a member there and once even offered me a ride back to Dearborn on his personal plane. During the flight, Mr. Ford's friends—none of whom were Ford Motor Company employees—asked him what I did for the corporation.

"Chase tells me what kind of cars we should build in the future, what they should cost, and what the selling price should be," Mr. Ford replied. "He tells me how many cars we should make and sets the production schedule. He also works on the budgets for all the Ford facilities."

I would later become friends with many of those people, and that conversation remained a standing joke. They would always say that it sound like I, not Mr. Ford, was the one really running the company!

That flight was memorable for another reason, too. On the way back from Seminole, we ran into a major snowstorm, and the plane was forced to land in the tiny town of Findlay, Ohio. All of us, including Mr. Ford, made our way to the only hotel in town. Most of the rooms shared a common bath, but as I was traveling with my wife, we were given one of the only rooms with a private one. When we went downstairs for breakfast the next morning, we were surprised to see a huge crowd gathered outside the hotel. Word had gotten out that Henry Ford II was staying there, and it seemed like everybody for miles around had come to the hotel for a glimpse of the famous tycoon.

The Ford Motor Company sent cars down for everyone later that day and drove us back to Michigan.

Over the years, it became clear to me that Henry Ford II was increasingly skeptical about my work ethic. Ford always wondered aloud how I could be such a good golfer and still have time to work as hard as people told him I did. It didn't help when he turned on his television one Sunday afternoon and saw me—on a rare vacation—playing with golf-legend Gary Player in Bing Crosby's National Pro-Am Golf Championship in Pebble Beach. On live television, Bing said I was a friend of his and mentioned that we played golf together at Seminole. Mr. Ford is reported to have exclaimed, "What in the hell is Chase doing out there when he's supposed to be working?!"

Word of the incident soon spread through the executive ranks in Dearborn, and many of my colleagues were afraid to play golf after that, for fear that Mr. Ford would find out.

><><

I had always loved convertibles, but I had never owned one, because my family always fretted about their safety.

"If you roll over in one of those things, you'll get killed," my parents used to say. But that didn't stop me from wanting one.

As I learned more about automobiles and how they were put together, I became convinced that there had to be a better way to make a convertible—a way to build a car with a retractable top that offered the rollover protection of a standard hardtop. So I started asking Engineering about the possibility of building a convertible with a retractable metal roof instead of the conventional soft-top. I was surprised to learn that the guys in Ford's Advanced Styling Studio, led by A.G. "Gil" Spear, were already working on one. The engineers in the company's Special Projects Division were, too. They were trying to come up with a mechanism for a retractable hardtop for the super-secret Continental Mark II.

The Continental Mark II was the Ford Motor Company's attempt to build the ultimate American luxury car. It was designed to challenge the highest-end Cadillacs and Chryslers and leave them in its dust. Work on the car had begun in 1952, but I didn't learn about it until September 1954. I also learned about a secret marketing study conducted by the newly formed Continental Division that found that customers who could afford it were willing to pay a premium of more than 30 percent for a convertible with a retractable hardtop.

That was all the ammunition I needed to make my pitch for a Ford version. At my urging, Engineering began trying to adapt the Continental mechanism for the '57 Ford. When they demonstrated the prototype for McNamara in November, he became an enthusiastic supporter of the project. The Continental Division cancelled its plans for a retractable-hardtop version of the Mark II, deciding that it was too complicated. But we moved forward with ours.

The retractable hardtop was neither simple nor cheap.[57] The mechanism itself was difficult to build, and it required major modifications to the car itself. Even with the longer wheelbase, the Fairlane required a longer rear deck, a new frame, and many other structural modifications to accommodate the bulky roof mechanism. It was a Rube Goldberg design, but it worked. And I knew the cars would be showstoppers when they made their debut.

⋈

When the '57 Fords were unveiled in October 1956, they proved to be just that. In many ways, these cars were the culmination of everything I had worked for in Product Planning. The cars we were selling were now no longer simply basic transportation. They were longer, wider, and lower than ever before, sporting sharply creased, new styling. The company had invested $610 million in this makeover.[58] Customers had their

---

57 The fully automatic roof mechanism used seven electric motors, eight breakers, ten relays, thirteen switches, and 610 feet of wire.
58 "The Cellini of Chrome," *Time*, Vol. 70, No. 19 (Nov. 4, 1957), p. 101.

choice of eighteen different body styles and trim levels, ranging from the entry-level two-door Custom to the elegant Sunliner convertible.

In the late 1950s, bigger was definitely better as far as most Americans were concerned, and Fords were now among the biggest automobiles in their class. The top-of-the-line Fairlane 500 was half a foot longer than the previous version and almost eight inches longer than Chevrolet's competing model, the Bel Air. Even the Custom was larger than the base model Chevrolet in every dimension except overall height. Remarkably, the extra size came at only a very modest price premium. Thanks to Engineering's clever interchangeability plan, most Fairlane 500 models cost only about forty dollars more than the comparable but smaller Bel Air, while the Sunliner convertible was actually six dollars *cheaper* than a convertible Bel Air. Ford's advertising characterized the base model as "the fine car for half the fine-car price."[59]

All of the new Fords, particularly the high-end Fairlanes, were well received. Though a few reviewers grumbled that the long-wheelbase models were hard to park, a survey of owners by *Popular Mechanics* found that nearly 98 percent of buyers liked the extra length.[60] Dealers loved the new Fords, too. They were happy we were finally giving them something to really get ahead of Chevrolet. The stylish Sunliner convertible was the industry's best-selling '57 ragtop.[61] It was a beautiful car. That long wheelbase and the big fin cresting the long rear fenders—it was so different from the regular, stodgy Ford! But the *pièce de résistance* was the retractable hardtop. Though it was not ready for production until February 1957 and did not go on sale until April, it proved to be a real home run. The first production car was delivered to President Dwight D. Eisenhower on April 14.

Although Ford's ad agency, J. Walter Thompson, had suggested various names for the new model, we finally opted for *Skyliner*—a name

---

59 "Buy a FORD and Bank the Difference," advertisement, *The Saturday Evening Post* (c. 1957), reprinted in *The Hemmings Motor News Book of Postwar Fords*, p. 85.

60 "Owners Report: How Good Is the 1957 Ford?" *Popular Mechanics*, Vol. 107, No. 3 (March 1957), pp. 89–90.

61 Adler, p. 75. Sunliner sales for 1957 totaled 77,728 units; see Gunnell, p. 398.

previously used for cars equipped with an unusual, transparent Plexiglas roof panel. With a starting price of $2,942, the Skyliner was expensive. But its showroom appeal was second to none. Not even Cadillac had anything to match the Skyliner, and the fully automatic roof was a great conversation piece.

With its lofty price and late introduction, the Skyliner was not a huge seller. However, the rest of the '57 line set new sales records for Ford. Just as importantly, the '57 gave Ford its first unequivocal victory over Chevrolet since the end of the war. Ford had technically come out on top two times before, in 1947 and 1949, but only because of extended model years or strikes at GM. This time there were no major strikes, and Ford was still comfortably ahead for the model year, selling a record 1.67 million cars[62] to Chevrolet's 1.5 million.[63] The long-wheelbase Fairlane models played a major role in that success, accounting for almost 47 percent of Ford passenger car sales.[64]

By the time the 1957 models went on sale, I had left Product Planning for a new job as car marketing manager for the Ford Division. The dual-wheelbase strategy was abandoned in 1958, but only because Ford opted to standardize around the longer wheelbase. The full-size Ford would continue to grow and become even more luxurious throughout the next decade, culminating in the very popular and widely imitated LTD. That car, which was famously advertised as being quieter than a Rolls-Royce, would never have been possible if we had not already demonstrated so

62 James M. Flammang, David L. Lewis, and the Auto Editors of Consumer Guide: *Ford Chronicle: A Pictorial History from 1893* (Lincolnwood, Ill.: Publications International, 1992).

63 Different sources list differing figures for Chevrolet's 1957 model year production, ranging from 1,505,910 (the Auto Editors of Consumer Guide, *Encyclopedia of American Cars*, p. 885) to 1,508,931 (Arch Brown, "SIA Comparison Report: 1957 Chevrolet, Ford and Plymouth," reprinted in *The Hemmings Book of Postwar Fords*, p. 81) to 1,515,177 (Gunnell, *Standard Catalog of American Cars 1946–1975*, pp. 167–168).

64 Ford sold 148,725 Fairlanes and 637,161 Fairlane 500s for 1957, 46.9 percent of model-year production. See Gunnell, pp. 398–399.

conclusively that Ford could build a credible near-luxury car—and make a handsome profit doing so.

The retractable hardtop survived through 1959, selling a total of 48,394 units in three model years. There were quality problems after I left, because there wasn't anybody fighting for it. In the end, I think it was just discarded. The retractable-hardtop concept was revived in the 1990s by Mercedes and Mitsubishi and is now offered by a number of automakers.

As with the Thunderbird, Product Planning only deserves part of the credit for these legendary automobiles. A big share of the credit goes to Styling and Engineering. But I still consider the '57 Fords to be the high-water mark of my Product Planning career. Friends still ask me where they can find one—particularly a Fairlane 500 Sunliner convertible. These cars may not have been as iconic as the Thunderbird, but in terms of both volume and profitability, they were even greater hits.

When I left Product Planning at the end of 1956, my staff decided to throw me a send-off: a Chase Morsey Day of their own. The guys all got together for lunch with me and put together a presentation. They all knew how much I relied on those forty-by-sixty boards and had Charlie Gara—the man who did all the artwork for the department—prepare a bunch of them for the occasion, with cartoons poking fun at various things that had happened during my time as product planning manager. The first chart said, "The Man Behind Marketing the Ford in Your Future: Just a Few Glimpses into the Business Career of Chase Morsey Jr." The last one was a photograph of the taillights of a '56 Chevrolet. "Look out, Chevy," the caption read. "Chase is coming!"

Chapter Seven

AROUND THE
WORLD IN A FORD

I became the car marketing manager for the Ford Division in the summer of 1956. It was a new position at the company, with the overall responsibility for sales promotion, sales training, and advertising for all of Ford's passenger cars. A separate position was created to handle Ford trucks, and it was filled by a new arrival from the company's Philadelphia sales office named Lee Iacocca.[65] Our boss was the Ford Division's newly appointed general sales manager, Charlie Beacham. Beacham was a good ol' boy from the South. He kept a barrel in his office marked "The Gonna Barrel." Anytime someone promised him that they were going to do something, he would frown and point to that barrel.

"Guys gonna do this and gonna do that," he'd say.

Lee was his favorite, no question about it. But I understood why. Charlie had previously been the regional sales manager in Philadelphia, where he had been very impressed with Iacocca's work—particularly his highly successful promotional campaign for the '56 Ford. That had done so well that it was subsequently adopted nationwide, resulting in

---

65 I do not recall the exact dates, but I probably started my new position within a few weeks of Lee Iacocca's promotion to truck-marketing manager, which came shortly before Iacocca's wedding to Mary McCleary in September 1956. See Lee Iacocca with William Novak, *Iacocca: An Autobiography* (New York: Bantam Books, 1984), p. 42.

thousands of extra sales.[66] Lee and I worked well together and later became good friends.

In my new role, I worked closely with Ford's advertising agency, J. Walter Thompson. Together, we were responsible for developing all of our print, television, radio, and outdoor ad campaigns. When I took over the relationship, many of Ford's senior managers were clamoring for a new ad agency. They had grown tired of J. Walter Thompson's work, believed the ads were focusing too much on the company as a whole and not enough on the Ford brand, and thought we could do better. I thought otherwise and quickly concluded that the agency had some of the best creative minds in the industry. I thought the real problem lay with Ford, not J. Walter Thompson. Until now, we had not established our own marketing department. As a result, the company's approach to advertising was scattershot and unfocused. There was no overarching philosophy or message, and no one in Dearborn was accountable for coordinating our marketing activity. I resolved to do better.

One of the first challenges I faced was overhauling Ford's television advertising. Ford had sponsored a series of TV shows since 1948, but their ratings had been consistently lackluster. The *Ford Festival*, a musical variety show starring noted opera singer James Melton, had been canceled after only one season. Its replacement, the half hour *Ford Television Theatre*, was not doing much better.[67] I asked the agency to come up with something completely different.

Dan Seymour, the head of J. Walter Thompson's Radio-Television Department,[68] suggested Ford sponsor a new show starring country music star Tennessee Ernie Ford. The popular singer had developed his hillbilly persona while working as a radio announcer in Southern California after the war. In the early 1950s, he had a string of country

---

66 Ibid, pp. 40–42.

67 This was a television version of a radio program Ford had sponsored from 1947 to 1949. The TV show debuted on NBC in October 1952, taking over the nine thirty in the evening Thursday time slot previously held by the *Ford Festival*.

68 Seymour joined J. Walter Thompson in 1955 and remained with the agency until 1974, eventually becoming its president.

hits that he had parlayed into a brief stint as the host of NBC's *Kollege of Musical Knowledge* and three memorable guest appearances on the hit CBS television series *I Love Lucy* in 1954 and 1955. That same year, he had topped the music charts with his rendition of Merle Travis's "Sixteen Tons," still an icon of mid-1950s popular music. I wasn't a big fan of country music, but I was a big fan of Tennessee Ernie Ford. The way he approached it was different. It was exciting, and I thought we at the Ford Motor Company could tap into that excitement. I believed he would attract a lot of viewers, and I knew that would translate into a bigger audience for our ads. The play on names—Ford and Ford—probably didn't hurt either, although I never thought about it in those terms at the time. I convinced Ford's Advertising Committee to sponsor the new series.

The first episode of *The Ford Show*—better known as *The Tennessee Ernie Ford Show*—aired October 4, 1956, on NBC, guest starring Reginald Gardiner and Greer Garson. It was a hit. The series quickly become one of the highest-rated shows on TV, consistently placing among the top ten most watched programs. The series lasted through the 1960–61 season, and I think it helped us score a lot of points with consumers. I also thought it was pretty entertaining!

Another advertising success during my stint as car marketing manager was a television and radio campaign that married a familiar Ford marketing slogan to a popular new song. I had heard Frank Loesser's "Standing on the Corner" on the radio and thought it was a catchy tune.[69]

I suggested that we license the rights to the song and change the lyrics of the refrain from "watching the girls go by" to "watching the Fords go by," which had been a Ford advertising tag line since the introduction

---

69 "Standing on the Corner" was written and composed by Frank Loesser for his musical comedy *The Most Happy Fella*, which opened on Broadway in May 1956 and lasted 676 performances. Columbia Records released a version of the song, performed by The Four Lads, as a single about two months before the show opened, to great success.

of the Model T. The combination made for a memorable series of TV and radio spots.

I also developed direct-mail campaigns, which were a first for the Ford Division. Remembering the success I'd had with direct-mail marketing back at Amherst, I decided to see how consumers would respond to a similar effort from an automaker. I didn't want to limit it to Ford customers either; I wanted to go after Chevrolet owners as well.

Ford's market research manager, Bob Eggert, and I sat down and figured out how to do it. J. Walter Thompson helped develop and implement it, but we were the ones who spent hours kicking around ideas and figuring out what to say. We decided to offer prizes, like a plastic scale model of the Thunderbird, to anyone who went to a local Ford dealer and took a test drive. Later campaigns offered a chance to win even bigger prizes and came in envelopes emblazoned with the tantalizing tag line, "You may have won…" that was later popularized by the Publishers Clearing House Sweepstakes.

One thing that made my job as Ford's car marketing manager a little easier, at least initially, was the company's success in NASCAR—something I'd helped put in motion when I was still in Product Planning.

Ford had never paid much attention to stock car racing, but Chevrolet sure did. They saw victory on those old dirt tracks as a way of promoting their new V-8. They quickly realized that a win on Sunday translated into sales on Monday—at least in the South. Chevrolet's advertising agency, Campbell-Ewald, capitalized on this by christening the Chevy car "the Hot One." It was a smart move, and I would have done the same thing if I were in charge of Chevrolet's marketing. But as a Ford man, I knew that—just like the Corvette—this was a move that demanded an aggressive response from us.

As I said, there was little interest in stock car racing among Ford's executives and engineers, but I argued that we owed it to our dealers in the South to get in the game. So Ford established its own racing team. It was financed by the Ford Division and initially overseen by the company's Engineering staff, but it was officially owned by former Indianapolis 500 winner Pete DePaolo.

It did not get off to a great start. As talented as the Ford engineers were, they had no experience with the brutal demands of stock car racing. In those days, most of the races were still held on dirt tracks, which had a habit of eating up even the best of cars.[70] There was also considerable tension between Ford's engineers and the more seasoned race mechanics employed by the team. During our first six months of competition, mechanical failures and technical disqualifications were frequent. Victories were few and far between, greatly limiting the racing program's publicity value for Ford. I knew we had to do something to turn it around.

During the Daytona Speed Weeks in February 1956, I dispatched the Ford Division's special projects manager, Joe MacKay, to Florida to assess the situation. When he returned, MacKay recommended taking the racing program out of the hands of Engineering.

"I think it might be wise for us to bring the management of the thing to the Ford Division, since it's our money that's being spent," he suggested.

"Just fix the damn thing, Joe," I said.

And he did.

MacKay was not a racing fan, but he was an adept problem-solver, and he understood exactly what I was hoping to accomplish with the program. With the help of John Holman, whom MacKay and DePaolo hired to run the NASCAR operation in May 1956, MacKay resolved many of the organizational conflicts and ensured that Ford's engineers gave the racers what they needed to start winning. He decided which events the Ford team should enter and worked with J. Walter Thompson to promote the results, and he kept me up to date on the progress. I trusted MacKay and gave him complete autonomy. I think we worked

---

70 Of the fifty-six NASCAR races held during the 1956 season, only eleven were held on paved tracks (See "NASCAR History: 'The Beginning,'" www.decadesofracing.net).

well together because I wasn't in his hair. I let him worry about the details.

MacKay invited me to watch my first race that summer when NASCAR came to Flat Rock in Michigan. I was a longtime fan of the Indianapolis 500, but I had never seen a stock car race and didn't know what to expect. In those days, the fastest drivers had to start at the back of the pack and work their way up to the front. I almost had a heart attack watching the Ford drivers, Curtis Turner and Joe Weatherly, pass all those other cars and come in first and second. I could see why NASCAR was developing such an enthusiastic following.

After I left Product Planning to take over Car Marketing, I continued to oversee MacKay's efforts. I asked that he continue to report to me, because I understood what a powerful marketing tool our increasingly successful racing team could become. By the start of the 1957 season, Ford was dominating all three NASCAR divisions: Grand National, Convertible, and Short Track. At the Grand National race at Florida's Titusville-Cocoa Airport on December 30, 1956, for example, the DePaolo Fords took first, second, third, and fourth places![71]

Winning those races was the equivalent of winning a big bowl game or even the World Series. In one important section of the country, it put Ford's name in every newspaper and on the lips of much of the car-buying public. The impact on sales was immediate and clear. It was as effective as any ad, so it was not surprising that our rivals at General Motors decided to put an end to it.

GM's chairman, Harlow Curtice, was also the head of the Automobile Manufacturers Association—the trade group that represented the nation's automakers. In February 1957, he introduced a resolution calling for all of the car companies to cease their support for and promotion of motorsports competition of any kind. The ostensible reason was safety, but I suspect the fact that we were beating the pants off Chevrolet

71 The Auto Editors of Consumer Guide, "1956 NASCAR Grand National Season Recap," HowStuffWorks.com, 31 July 2007, http://auto.howstuffworks.com/auto-racing/nascar/season-recaps/1950s/1956-nascar.htm.

in NASCAR had more to do with it. Racing was also expensive, and General Motors was spending a lot of money trying to keep up with us. I think they just wanted out.

Whatever the rationale, the AMA passed the racing ban on June 6, 1957, and Henry Ford II promptly sent out a memo that made it clear that all Ford executives were expected to abide by that resolution. We had no choice but to buy out the contracts of our racing personnel. But I made one more contribution to NASCAR before we pulled the plug. I arranged for Ford to sell its stockpile of racing parts to Holman and driver Ralph Moody. Over the next few years, their organization would become one of the most important constructors in stock car racing.

Although I did not participate in the development of the 1958 Fords, as car marketing manager I was charged with finding a way to sell them. It was an uphill battle. Aesthetically, the '58 Fords were widely considered to be a step backward from the popular 1957 models. To make matters worse, because of the AMA's racing ban earlier that year, Ford was not allowed to promote competition, horsepower, or performance. That didn't leave me with much to work with, but I was determined to move the metal. I asked the agency to pull out all the stops.

Marty Ransohoff, a cofounder of Filmways, the company that made television commercials for J. Walter Thompson and other advertising agencies, came to Detroit to see me and discuss plans for the introduction of the 1958 Ford car. He offered a timely idea. A movie adaptation of Jules Verne's *Around the World in Eighty Days* had just debuted and was a box-office smash, and that was his inspiration.

"Why don't we drive a '58 Ford around the world in eighty days?" Ransohoff suggested.

"Wow!" I exclaimed. "Could we really do it?"

"I think we can," he said.

Ransohoff explained how he would arrange for a film crew to follow the car and photograph it in all sorts of exotic settings and locals. That footage would be edited into a series of television spots that would follow the Ford's progress around the globe.

It was a compelling idea, but also a dangerous one. In those days, many parts of the world lacked anything resembling a paved road, and anti-American sentiment was growing. We called a meeting of the Advertising Committee, which included Henry Ford II, Ernest Breech, Robert McNamara, and other top executives, to discuss those concerns. Everyone agreed that a serious accident—or, worse, a deliberate attack on the car or the film crew—would be a public relations disaster. As Ransohoff said in his usual blunt manner, "We would be f——!"

McNamara turned to me and said, "It's up to you, Chase."

I thought the public would love it and decided that it was worth the risk. "It's too great an opportunity to turn down," I said.

That decided it. Lee Iacocca turned to Ransohoff and joked, "If the car doesn't come back, Chase is going to have to look for another job."

But the car did come back, eventually.

In July 1957, our little caravan set out from Dearborn and headed to New York. It consisted of two 1958 Fairlane 500 four-door prototypes, two four-wheel-drive Ford F-350 trucks to carry supplies, and a Ford station wagon to carry the camera crew.[72] There were four drivers, led by Danny Eames of DePaolo Engineering—the company that had run Ford's now-defunct racing program.

After arriving in the Big Apple, they crossed the Atlantic and made their way east through England, France, Switzerland, Yugoslavia, Greece, Turkey, Iran, Afghanistan, Pakistan, India, Burma, Malaya, Thailand, Cambodia, and South Vietnam. From there, it was just a quick jump to the Philippines and then home to the United States. But completing the trip in eighty days proved impossible.

The expedition actually took about three and half months to complete and cost more than a million dollars. Along the way, the crew encountered all manners of obstacles, from rampaging monkeys to

---

72 Michael Parris, *Fords of the Fifties* (Tucson, Ariz.: California Bill's Automotive Handbooks, 2000), p. 144–145.

raging sandstorms and even civil wars.[73] Fortunately, the two cars held up remarkably well on the punishing trip. It turned out great. With the footage and photographs from that journey we were able to put together dozens of television commercials and an array of exciting print advertising, like the one showing a Fairlane 500 tackling a muddy trail in Pakistan during a monsoon.[74] Even ads that didn't feature shots of the Fords abroad included a special logo showing a Ford car orbiting a stylized globe, with slogans such as "Proved and Approved around the World." Ford used the same theme for its TV ads, kicking off the campaign with a televised gala hosted by Hugh Downs, then the announcer on *The Jack Paar Show*, featuring the new Ford cars rolling out from behind an enormous globe. The whole effort proved to be huge success.

As for Marty Ransohoff, he went on to become a successful film and television producer, responsible for shows like *The Beverly Hillbillies* and *Green Acres*. He also produced forty-five films, including such well-known movies as *Catch-22*, *Jagged Edge*, and *Ice Station Zebra*. When I moved to California in 1977, he also became my neighbor and a very good friend.

I served as car marketing manager for about a year, but many of my innovations continued to influence the company for decades—just like the changes I made in Product Planning.

A big one was the way we introduced new products to our dealers. Broadway musicals were big back then, and I came up with the idea of putting on theatrical productions, complete with lavish musical numbers and wide-screen color films, as part of our launch programs. These were very well received and generated a lot of excitement.

---

73 Parris says the trip lasted 110 days, but Phil Remington, whom Danny Eames hired as the expedition's chief mechanic, recalled that it took 119. See Parris, p. 145–146, and Dick Martin, "The Danny Eames Story," *Rod and Custom*, June 2011. In the latter article, Eames incorrectly recalls that Lee Iacocca orchestrated the project.
74 "Ford's rugged body defied the world's toughest roads," advertisement [c. 1958], reprinted at AdClassix.com, http://www.adclassix.com/ads/58fordsedan.htm.

But the biggest thing I changed was Ford's attitude toward J. Walter Thompson. As I said, when I started in the Car Marketing Department, many of the executives in Dearborn were ready to start looking for another advertising agency. I had confidence in the team there though, and thanks to the success of the campaigns we ran that year, Ford decided to stick with them. J. Walter Thompson went on to create some of the most memorable advertising campaigns of the last half century, coining tag lines like "Have You Driven a Ford Lately?" and "Quality Is Job One." Now known simply as JWT, it remains the Ford Motor Company's primary ad agency today.

When I left Car Marketing to take over as sales manager for the automaker's all-important Detroit district, the top executives at J. Walter Thompson came out from New York to honor me with a big send-off dinner. I told them to keep up the good work and ignore the negative rumors coming from Dearborn. They wished me luck in my new assignment.

I would need it.

Chapter Eight

A BRUSH WITH THE LAW—AND THE LAWLESS

By 1957, I had been with the Ford Motor Company for nearly a decade, but all of my experience had been at the corporate headquarters in Dearborn. I had never worked in the field. I'd had regular contact with the Ford Dealer Council during my time in Product Planning, but I had never worked with the dealers directly. So about a year after I became car marketing manager, my bosses decided it was time to broaden my horizons. Just before the start of the 1958 model year, they reassigned me, putting me in charge of the most important sales district in the country: Detroit.[75]

In my new role as district sales manager, I was responsible for overseeing Ford's relationship with all of its franchise dealers in the region. My office was in Plymouth, at the same parts depot where I had made my dramatic presentation comparing the design costs of the Ford and Chevrolet cars back in 1949. I was responsible for about 150 dealerships in southern Michigan and northern Ohio. It was a high-profile assignment because of the proximity to the Ford Motor Company World Headquarters, and I knew that I would be under intense scrutiny from

---

75 Lee Iacocca replaced me as car marketing manager and took over marketing for both cars and trucks in early 1960.

the company's senior executives. Since I had never worked directly with car dealers before, both the franchisees and I were a little concerned!

That concern was magnified by the fact that 1958 was a difficult time for the entire automobile industry. The nation was slipping into a recession, and buyers were less than impressed with Detroit's latest offerings—particularly Ford's newest product, the Edsel. It would soon become one of the worst commercial disasters in history. But the rest of Ford's '58 lineup did not fare much better, with the notable exception of the new Thunderbird.[76] Sales fell more than 40 percent from 1957's record-setting level.[77]

I tried to help the dealers as best I could, but there wasn't much I could do. I remembered how when I was IBM, I had convinced successful customers to show prospective buyers how they were using our machines to improve their businesses, and that inspired me to try a similar tactic with the Ford dealers. I went to the most profitable franchises in my district and asked if I could share their profit-and-loss statements with the other dealers. I assured them that any identifying details would be removed first. They agreed. It helped the other store owners see that there were other ways to make money, such as service and parts, even if they weren't selling many cars and trucks.

⤬

While I did my best to help the dealers in my district, relations between the company and its franchisees were deteriorating. For several years, there had been allegations that Ford and the other U.S. automakers were forcing dealers to take cars and trucks that they knew they could not sell. Dealers also complained about restrictions on carrying multiple brands and the ability of carmakers to pull their franchises with impunity.

---

76 The four-seater nearly doubled the volume of the Thunderbird despite a late introduction and a list price that was over $1,000 more than a Fairlane 500 hardtop.

77 Ford's passenger car sales fell from 1,676,448 units for the 1957 model year to 987,945 units for 1958 model year. (See Gunnell, pp. 399–401).

The entire industry had come under intense scrutiny by the federal government over dealer trade practices. In 1955, complaints from former dealers prompted Senator Joseph C. O'Mahoney, a Democrat from Wyoming, to organize congressional hearings on the matter.[78] Henry Ford II and other senior executives were called to testify, and the resulting pressure from the federal government forced Ford to liberalize many of its dealer policies.

Dealers were now allowed to sell more than one brand, and their franchises could no longer be terminated without cause.[79] But the complaints continued. So in the summer of 1958, the U.S. Attorney's Office in Detroit convened a grand jury to investigate charges that Ford had forced dealers to accept more vehicles than they had ordered. The Ford Motor Company's general counsel, William T. Gossett, selected me to receive the federal subpoena.

I was surprised when he called and asked me to come over to his office.

"Oh hell!" I thought. "What have I done now?"

When Gossett told me the reason why he had summoned me, I was hardly reassured. I had never received a subpoena before in my life, and I wasn't happy about the prospect of receiving one now. To be honest, I was scared.

"Why me?" I asked.

"Frankly, none of us up here knows enough about how cars are ordered," he said. "So, I told the U.S. Attorney you should receive the subpoena. We think you'll do a good job, Chase."

My knowledge of automobile ordering process may have been the primary reason why Gossett and the other senior executives chose me, but he explained that my track record of making persuasive presentations on controversial issues played a part in the decision, too.

"You're on the firing line," Gossett continued. "Besides, Chase, you know how to talk to people."

---

78 "Senators Will Study Auto Sales Practices," *New York Times*, Dec. 26, 1955.
79 Brinkley, pp. 583–585.

"Fine, Bill," I said. After all, it was my job. I did know it better than anyone in the company. But that did not make it any easier to open the envelope from the U.S. Attorney's Office when it arrived.

I walked into the federal courthouse in downtown Detroit just before eleven in the morning on Friday, September 19.[80] Even though I come from a family of attorneys, the closest I had ever come to a courtroom was watching *Perry Mason* on television. I didn't know where the courthouse was, where to park, or what would happen after I walked in the door. I had no lawyer, and nobody from the Ford Motor Company was with me. I had never seen the U.S. Attorney, nor did I know anything about the background of any of the jurors. As my footsteps echoed down the marble corridor that led to the courtroom, I couldn't help thinking about the consequences of a misstep here. What if I said the wrong thing and ended up hurting Ford? What if I ended up hurting myself? After all, the U.S. Attorney had called this hearing because he was not satisfied with the answers Mr. Ford had given in Washington. All of these thoughts were in my mind as I entered the courtroom and eyed the big bronze federal seal mounted on the wall.

My heart was racing as I took the stand. I hazarded a quick glance at the jury, trying to read their faces. What did they think about big corporations like Ford? I couldn't tell. The next thing I knew, I was raising my right hand and swearing to tell the truth, the whole truth, and nothing but the truth.

Then the questioning began. When it did, the fear I felt about saying the wrong thing became a source of strength. I was still scared, but I felt a growing sense of confidence as I answered one question after another. My fear made everything suddenly clear: I knew what I had to do. I had to defend the Ford Motor Company. I had to make it clear to the jurors and the Department of Justice that the automaker was not forcing its cars and trucks on its dealers. I spent the morning carefully explaining the dealer ordering and inventory process in great detail. I spent the

---

80 I still have my copy of the subpoena.

afternoon sparring with the U.S. attorney, who kept trying to trip me up. He was unsuccessful.

"A dealer can't make any money if he doesn't have cars to sell," I kept telling him.

He kept insinuating that Ford was pushing dealers to order more vehicles than they could move.

"Do you force cars on dealers?" the attorney asked.

"I wouldn't say we force cars on dealers, but there are times when dealers get overstocked," I said.

He cited specific examples of dealers who had too many cars left on their lots at the end of a particular month.

"Sometimes the dealers get overstocked because they don't sell as many cars as they anticipated." I shrugged. "So when it comes time to submit their next order, they simply cut back. That is standard procedure for dealers in the Detroit district. In addition, we have an inventory of all the cars in the district to help dealers make a sale, because the dealer might not have the color or model wanted by the customer."

I told the grand jury that they could talk to any dealer in my district and would hear the same thing.

The man from the Justice Department kept at it. I was getting tired of repeating myself, and I tried to come up with another way of putting it that the jurors would understand. I thought back to my time at the D.E. Sanford Company and how I would stop in at the Famous-Barr department store in downtown St. Louis to make sure they had enough product to sell.

"It's just like going into a department store. If the stuff you want isn't there, you'll go to another store," I said, turning to the jury box. "The dealer can't make a sale if he doesn't have any cars to sell."

I could see that the jurors understood when I put it in those terms. Several of them nodded in agreement.

Apparently, my testimony was enough for the grand jury. The matter was dissolved a few days later, without bringing anything to trial.

I never heard anything more about it, and I never saw another mention of it in the newspaper.

I was relieved to have the whole grand jury thing behind me, but I was soon confronted with an even more uncomfortable situation. It started with a call from John S. Bugas, Ford's vice president in charge of industrial relations. He was our point man with the unions, and he asked me to come right over to his office in Dearborn to discuss a very delicate matter.

"Chase, you have a young man in the south part of your district who owns a dealership that is failing," he said. "You've got to get this kid making some money."

I told Bugas I would see what I could do, but I asked what so special about this dealer.

"His father is the leader of the Purple Gang," Bugas said with a grimace, as he proceeded to tell me that the local organized crime syndicate had ties to the United Auto Workers union. [81] "We're involved in some very difficult contract negotiations right now with the UAW. If his dealership goes under that might hurt those talks. We need them to be on our side in the upcoming labor negotiations."

I told Bugas I understood. I knew that he was very familiar with organized crime in Detroit, because he had spent six years as special agent in charge of the FBI's Detroit field office prior to joining Ford.

---

81 The original Purple Gang was a primarily Jewish gang founded in Detroit around 1919. During Prohibition, the Purples became a major power in the Detroit underworld through their control of rum-running along the Detroit River, subsequently branching out into other criminal enterprises. Crime historians believe that by 1935, most of the original Purple Gang was defunct—some of its members having been killed or imprisoned, others leaving town or becoming part of other gangs. But the Purples' notoriety was such that the name remained almost synonymous with Detroit's organized crime. See Paul R. Kaviefi "Detroit's Infamous Purple Gang," *The Detroit News*, July 16, 1999, and "Mobsters, Mayhem & Murder," *The Times Magazine*, No. 34 (May 2007). According to investigative reporter Scott M. Burnstein, the post-Prohibition mob, commonly known as "The Detroit Combination" or "The Partnership," was largely Italian.

By the end of the day, I had recruited the best general manager I could find in the district. I didn't tell him what he was getting into. I just told him, "Look, this young kid needs help. Go down there, and see what you can do. It's important that he succeed."

You can believe I kept a close eye on things, checking in at least two or three times a week. The general manager I picked had a good record, but I didn't know him. He could have turned out to be terrible. He and the mobster's son might not have gotten along, or the dealership might still have gone broke, despite everybody's best efforts. There were at least half a dozen ways the situation could have gone sideways, and if it did, I was going to be the one on the hook—not just with Ford but also with the young man's father. I lost a good bit of sleep over the situation. But luckily for me, the general manager was excellent. Within three months, he succeeded in turning the business around. John Bugas was a very happy man. So was the young man's father.

On Christmas Eve, I was at my home in Grosse Pointe Shores, preparing to celebrate the holiday with my family. My mother had come up from St. Louis for the occasion. We were just sitting down to dinner when a long, black Cadillac limousine pulled into the driveway. One of my children alerted us to the unexpected arrival, and I pulled back the curtains just as two burly figures emerged from the idling vehicle. They looked like they had just stepped out of a particularly lurid gangster movie. I swallowed hard.

"Oh my God!" cried my mother, suddenly beside me. "They're coming to rob us!"

Instead, they knocked politely on the front door.

"Our boss would like to talk to you," one said, nodding toward the waiting limousine.

My family looked on in terror as I followed the hoods down the driveway. I would be lying if I said my heart wasn't racing just a little bit as I approached the black Cadillac and watched the second thug open the door and gesture for me to step inside. There I came face to face with the head of the most notorious criminal gang in Detroit. He smiled.

"Chase, I want to thank you for what you have done for my son," he said. "I'd like to give you money, like I do with most people, or at least an expensive present. But I've checked you out, and I know you wouldn't take it. However, I have a winery in Italy, and I brought you two cases of red wine made by my family. I would like to give you this wine as a Christmas present."

"I would be honored to accept it," I said.

The mob boss snapped his fingers, and one of his associates opened the trunk, took out two cases of wine, carried them to my front door, and set them down in the foyer. I shook hands with the local godfather and watched with no small amount of relief as he and his henchmen drove away.

All of my friends were astonished when I told them the story. They were amazed that I had dared to get in the car and risked being "taken for a ride," as they used to say in the movies. The truth was I was more startled than intimidated. I knew I had done right by the man's son, and I knew he had no reason to be mad at me. Of course, if that kid's dealership had gone under, it would have been a different story! But the whole scene sure left a lasting impression on my family. My mother never got over it. She lived to be ninety-eight, and she would always talk about the night those thugs came to the front door.

The remainder of my two-year tenure as Detroit district sales manager was less exciting but no less successful. The last year I was there, 1960, we achieved the highest percentage over Chevrolet of any district in the country. And we did it without forcing any cars on our dealers. I always told my guys, "We can beat Chevrolet, because we have better cars. We don't need to play any games."[82]

---

82 Both 1959 and 1960 were considerably better for Ford than 1958 had been: The Ford Division sold nearly 1.5 million passenger cars for the 1959 model year and 1.44 million for 1960. See Gunnell, pp. 400–405.

Chapter Nine

TEEING UP
LINCOLN

In early 1960, Robert McNamara called me into his office. By now, McNamara was Ford's executive vice president, and he would soon be named president of the company.[83]

"Chase, we want you to be the head of marketing for Lincoln-Mercury," he said.

I groaned inwardly. This was far from a plum assignment. The Lincoln-Mercury Division was in bad shape following several years of unpopular styling, poor sales, and organizational chaos. About five years earlier, Jack Reith and Lewis Crusoe had convinced Ford's Executive Committee to split Lincoln and Mercury into separate divisions, as part of a diversification strategy that also included setting up the ill-fated Edsel and Continental divisions. The whole thing was a disaster, and it cost both men their jobs. Crusoe had retired for health reasons in May 1957, and Reith was fired three months later. I was sad to see him go, though I knew it was the only way it could end. Now all four brands had been merged back into a single division, which reverted back to Lincoln-Mercury after the cancellation of the Edsel in November 1959. But that had not solved the underlying problems of poor styling and managerial mayhem. Mercury's 1960 sales were hovering at less than half their 1956 volume, and the enormous 1958–1960 Lincolns were losing so much

---

83 McNamara was appointed president of the Ford Motor Company in November 1960, but served only a short time before resigning to become Secretary of Defense for the newly elected Kennedy administration.

money that McNamara had actually thought about killing the brand in 1958. My assignment to the Detroit district had allowed me to avoid all this political strife at World Headquarters, but I knew enough about what had been going on not to relish a return to Dearborn.

"Bob, I don't want to work for Lincoln-Mercury," I told McNamara. "I'm a Ford guy."

But McNamara was ready for me.

"That's OK, Chase. We have an opening for a district manager in Newark," he said without missing a beat. "We'd be happy to transfer you."

I felt like a sitting duck. As McNamara clearly suspected, I was even less interested in moving to New Jersey than I was in working for Lincoln-Mercury. I reluctantly accepted my new assignment.

When I arrived, the big news at Lincoln-Mercury was the midyear launch of the compact Mercury Comet. Based on Ford's new Falcon, which had debuted a few months earlier, the Comet was originally conceived as a new Edsel. However, when the Edsel brand was discontinued in late 1959, Lincoln-Mercury was forced to hastily scrap the Edsel badges and discard most of the catalogs, advertisements, and promotional materials that had already been ordered for the new car. I had to start from scratch. They didn't have anything, but I worked with our film company—Wilding Pictures—to put together a short movie to send around to all the dealers to help build some buzz for the Comet. I also developed a direct-mail campaign to promote the new car.

Fortunately, I had a strong product to work with. The Comet was closely related to the Falcon mechanically, but it was more attractive and desirable in many respects. While the Falcon was efficient and economical, it had been engineered to extremely strict cost and weight restrictions; scarcely a dollar or pound was wasted on frills. The Comet, conceived as a more upscale model, was longer and somewhat heavier, with nicer interior materials, a softer ride, and a formal roof line, like that of the Thunderbird or the big Galaxie. It was a much better car than the Falcon, and it only cost seventy to eighty dollars more.

It was the first time in years that the Lincoln-Mercury Division had a better car than Ford. I knew that the Lincoln-Mercury dealers felt like neglected stepchildren, so I really played up the advantages of the Comet to make them feel like their day had finally come. It worked, but I also succeeded in upsetting some of my former Ford colleagues. They feared that the Comet would hurt Falcon sales, and they were right. I remember that a couple of the regional sales managers of Ford, who were friends of mine, got really upset about how hard we were pushing the Comet.

"Lincoln-Mercury's got a lot more problems than you do," I told them.[84]

The Comet was also better than any compact car General Motors had in its stable at that time. Despite the late introduction, the Comet sold quite well, accounting for nearly 40 percent of Lincoln-Mercury's total volume for the model year.

The final months of the 1960 model year were marred by a sad occasion: the funeral of my old friend Jack Reith, who passed away on July 3 at the age of forty-five. We had seen less of each other in recent years, particularly after Reith moved to Cincinnati, Ohio, to become president of the Crosley Division of Avco Manufacturing Corporation. But Reith's death was a real blow. After all, he and I had been friends since the war, and it was Reith who had brought me to Ford in the first place.

He had been my first friend in Detroit. Reith looked after me during my early years at Ford, when it was important to have a protector. He knew I loved to play golf, and we would play together a couple of Saturdays each month. Reith would have me as his guest, and he would invite my wife and me over to his house for dinner afterward. He was a real good friend, and if it hadn't been for him, I never would have had

---

84 Ford subsequently developed its own plush version of the Falcon, the Futura, which debuted midway through the 1961 model year. See "The Falcon Futura," *Motor Trend*, Vol. 14, No. 6 (June 1961).

the opportunity to work for this great company that I felt so passionately about.

><><

With the Comet off to a great start, I turned my attention to Lincoln. For the 1961 model year, Lincoln dropped all of its previous models in favor of a trimmer, sleeker new Continental. It was McNamara's idea, and it was a good one. The new Lincoln's elegant styling, originally conceived as a design study for the 1961 Thunderbird,[85] was much admired—even winning a bronze medal from the prestigious Industrial Design Institute, which seldom paid much attention to Detroit products. However, although the new Lincoln was a fine car, the brand's prestige had shrunk considerably in recent years. Its sales were just a fraction of Cadillac's.[86] My challenge was to put Lincoln back on the map and get well-heeled buyers back into Lincoln-Mercury showrooms.

I developed a variety of tactics, including a direct-mail promotion that received a remarkable 30 percent response, but I knew what Lincoln really needed was greater visibility among America's elite. I had to figure out a way to associate Lincolns with upscale venues. As an avid golfer myself, I could think of nothing better than the country club. After all, that was where our target customers hung out. I belonged to several prestigious country clubs, and I had a lot of connections in the golf world. So I came up with the idea of giving Lincolns to golf pros to drive to tournaments. The practice is commonplace today. But if someone had done it before, I had never heard about it.

The next step was television. In 1962, I contacted Mark McCormack, the attorney for the prominent golf pros Arnold Palmer and Gary Player, and explained what I was trying to do. We put together a weekly TV

---

85 The '61 Continental originated in Elwood Engel's advanced studio in 1958, developed by Engel, Colin Neale, John Orf, and Bob Thomas. Intended as a possible replacement for the 1958–1960 Ford Thunderbird, the original clay model was a two-door hardtop, although the production car was somewhat larger and offered as either a four-door sedan or a four-door convertible. See Lamm and Holls, pp. 149–150.

86 For the 1961 model year, for example, Lincoln-Mercury sold 25,164 Lincoln Continentals, while Cadillac sales totaled 138,379. See Gunnell, pp. 126–127 and p. 501.

series called *Challenge Golf*, in which Player and Palmer would take on two different pros each week in a series of matches at some of America's leading country clubs. The matches were to be recorded in advance and broadcasted on Saturday afternoons. I flew out to Los Angeles to oversee the start of production.

The first episode, which aired on ABC in January 1963,[87] was filmed at the Riviera Country Club in the posh Los Angeles suburb of Pacific Palisades. It was followed by episodes shot at the Los Angeles and Bel-Air Country Clubs. After the Bel-Air show, I asked the production people when we were going up to Pebble Beach. The golf course at Pebble Beach was one of the most famous in the nation and one with which I was quite familiar. I had been there in January, when Gary Player and I had competed in the 1963 Crosby Pro-Am. During the initial negotiations with the Revue executives, I had specifically requested Pebble Beach as a location, but to my surprise, the producers told me they had no intention of going there. Revue preferred to shoot all the episodes at courses in the greater Los Angeles area, to save money. I protested that we had clearly discussed filming at Pebble Beach, but the producers were adamant.

"It's not in our contract," they insisted.

Frustrated, I called Ford's general counsel, who reviewed the agreement and found that it said nothing at all about venues.

"Chase, I've got the contract in my hands," he said. "Pebble Beach is not listed."

While Revue may have been within its legal rights, I was still not satisfied, so I decided to put in a call to the chairman of Revue's parent company, MCA: legendary agent and movie mogul Lew Wasserman. I had never met Wasserman before, and I doubted he knew who I was, but I was determined to shoot at Pebble Beach. I knew I probably wouldn't even get through, but I had no other options. Imagine my surprise when the switchboard operator at MCA connected me to Wasserman's office.

---

87 A company called Rare Sportsfilms Inc. now offers some of these episodes on DVD (www. raresportsfilms.com/ chall11.html).

I was soon speaking to the chairman himself. When he came on the phone, I was almost speechless—*almost*.

"Look, you probably don't realize it, but we've got a problem with Revue," I told Wasserman. "During the preliminary discussions, before they wrote up the contract, I specifically told them I wanted to go up to Pebble Beach. Now they say it's too expensive to shoot up there. They told me it wasn't in the contract, and they're right—it isn't in the contract. But we sure talked about it beforehand. I would appreciate it if you would see if there is something you could do so that we could shoot one of the matches at Pebble Beach."

"I'll look into it and get back to you," Wasserman said.

It was a very frank conversation, and in retrospect, I was amazed at my own confidence in confronting this titan of Hollywood. It was kind of like that first big meeting with the senior executives at Ford—I just didn't know enough to be scared! If I had thought it through, I probably wouldn't have bothered. Fortunately, I just went with my gut, which had rarely steered me wrong.

Wasserman was true to his word. He met with the producers and demanded to know if they had led me to believe we would be filming in Pebble Beach. The producers reluctantly admitted that they had. Wasserman told them to apologize to me and make things right. They did as they were told, and the first Pebble Beach match—pitting Palmer and Player against Byron Nelson and Ken Venturi—aired on Saturday, March 30, 1963. It was really a coup to have all those outstanding players on one show.

Far from being annoyed with me, Wasserman seemed bemused by the whole incident. He took a liking to me, and when I'd see him at parties and social functions years later, he'd say, "I know you; you're the guy who made me take the golfers up to Pebble Beach."[88]

Player, Palmer, and McCormack also remained my friends and periodic golfing partners long after the show ended. Gary and I would play

---

88 The whole saga was later written up as a chapter in Mark McCormack's book, *The Terrible Truth About Lawyers: How Lawyers Work and How to Deal with Them* (Sag Harbor, New York: Beech Tree Books, 1987).

the two of them the week before the annual Bing Crosby tournament. I don't think they ever beat us. We'd make little bets. In fact, I still have a twenty-dollar bill, signed by Arnold Palmer, that says, "Chase, don't spend this too quick, I'll be back."

My idea of associating Lincoln with the world of professional golf proved to be a big success. The country club set loved it, and that was precisely who I was trying to reach. Once they got used to the sight of their favorite touring pros emerging from our luxurious automobiles, Lincoln's reputation began to rebound. Today, luxury brands vie with one another to ink endorsement deals with players like Tiger Woods and Greg Norman.

As for me, I was soon on to bigger and better things. In late 1962, I received my last assignment at the Ford Motor Company, when I was promoted to head of marketing for the Ford Division. Before I left, the Lincoln-Mercury National Dealer Council sent me a letter, signed by all of its members, thanking me for "the many considerations, courtesies, and the job well done by you in our behalf." It was a remarkable gesture, given the frequently adversarial relationships between automakers and their dealer councils. None of my predecessors had ever received such accolades. I still have a framed copy of this letter on my desk.

CHAPTER TEN

SELLING PONIES

In the fall of 1963, I returned to the Ford Division as general marketing manager. It would be my last assignment at the Ford Motor Company but one of the most rewarding. In my new capacity, I reported to my old colleague Lee Iacocca, who had become vice president and general manager of the Ford Division in November 1960. I was pleased to be working with Lee again, because he was smart as hell. I thought he was terrific and knew we would make a great team. And we did—particularly when it came time to launch one of Ford's most important cars since the Model T: the Mustang.

A stylish, attainable, sporty car with broad appeal, the Mustang was, in many ways, the spiritual successor of the two-seat Thunderbird. In fact, before the Mustang name was formally approved, Henry Ford II seriously considered calling the new car the Thunderbird II.

Over the years, Ford had received many letters asking for the return of the "Little Bird." Early in the Mustang's development, the Budd Company actually proposed reviving the '57 T-Bird using the original dies and a modified Ford Falcon platform.[89] But Iacocca was not interested in simply rehashing the original Thunderbird. His plan, developed by an informal group of Ford executives known as the Fairlane Committee, who met weekly at Dearborn's Fairlane Inn, called for an

---

89 Frank Taylor, "Thunderbird: Three Years of Glory, 1955–1957," *Car Classics* (February 1975).

entirely new car—one aimed at the young baby boomers, whom Ford market researchers had noted would begin reaching driving age by the mid-1960s.[90]

I was not part of Iacocca's original Fairlane Committee, as some authors have written,[91] but the studies that shaped the group's thinking had their roots in the work I had done several years earlier, when I was car marketing manager. When I returned to Ford in 1963, the Mustang's design had already been approved, and the car's mechanical development was well underway. Job One—the start of regular retail production—was slated for March 9, 1964.[92] My role was to oversee the marketing and sales campaigns being put together to support the launch of this important new product. It would be one of the biggest advertising blitzes in automotive history.

We spent $10 million to promote the Mustang and employed many innovative marketing strategies. For example, shortly before the Mustang's launch in mid-April 1964, Ford loaned new Mustangs to hundreds of radio disc jockeys and college newspaper editors. We knew they would love the car, and we were pretty sure they would let their listeners and readers know it. We were right.

Even before the Mustang went on sale, it was prominently featured at the New York World's Fair, which opened to the public on April 22. Tying the Mustang's launch to the opening of the 1964 World's Fair was Lee's idea and had been part of the marketing plan for the car since the beginning. Ford spent some $30 million constructing its pavilion for the fair, with exhibits and mechanical features designed by WED Enterprises, Inc., a subsidiary of the Walt Disney Company. A dozen

---

90 Donald N. Frey, whom Lee Iacocca had appointed to my old job in November 1960, played a major role in those discussions. See Robert A. Fria, *Mustang Genesis: The Creation of the Pony Car* (Jefferson, N.C.: McFarland & Co., Inc., 2010), pp. 56-59 and Halberstam, pp. 369–370.

91 A number of sources incorrectly identify me as a member of the Fairlane Committee (e.g., Michael Lamm, "First Mustang: Trendsetter of the 1960s," *Special Interest Autos*, No. 24 (September–October 1974)). However, most of the group's meetings took place between 1960 and 1962, while I was still at Lincoln-Mercury.

92 The production design for the Mustang was approved on September 10, 1962. See Fria, p. 67 and 121.

Mustang convertibles were modified by Carron & Co. for use in the Disney-engineered Magic Skyway ride, in which 146 new Ford convertibles took visitors through a series of "time tunnels" into displays of prehistoric and futuristic worlds, brought to life by Disney's unique "Audio-Animatronic" technology.[93] Walt Disney himself cut the ribbon to open the Ford Wonder Rotunda.

The Mustang was also on display alongside other current Ford models in the Pavilion's Product Salon. During the fair's six-month run in 1964, the Ford Pavilion attracted 6.8 million visitors, with 8.1 million more in 1965.[94] I worked with WED Enterprises during the development of the Ford Pavilion and came to know Walt Disney quite well prior to his death in December 1966. Disney's Walt Disney World Resort, and later Disney's Epcot Center, used some of the same technology originally developed for the 1964 New York World's Fair.

I knew the car-buying public was not the only audience we needed to get excited about the Mustang. Recalling my past success using Broadway-style shows to build dealer enthusiasm, I commissioned Wilding Pictures to develop a special musical extravaganza to get Ford salesmen primed for the launch of the Mustang. The show ran in at least seven major markets.[95]

The Mustang was one of the boldest designs ever to come out of Detroit, and I wanted to make sure people recognized that. So in early 1964, I approached Walter Hoving, chairman of the famous New York jeweler Tiffany & Co., about the possibility of creating a special design award for the Mustang. Tiffany's had never given a design award to a commercial product before, but Hoving and the other Tiffany executives were very receptive to my proposal and thought it was a good idea. Once

---

93 Anderson, "New York World's Fair" and Ford Motor Company/WED Enterprises, Inc., "Welcome to the Ford Motor Company Pavilion," *VIP Souvenir Book: 1964 New York World's Fair,* reprinted at 1964/1965 New York World's Fair, ed. Bill Young, http://nywf64.com/ford03.shtml.

94 Anderson, "New York World's Fair."

95 Historian Randy Leffingwell says there were thirteen of these shows, but I only remember seven. See Leffingwell, *Mustang: America's Classic Pony Car* (Ann Arbor, Mich.: Lowe & B. Hould Pub., 1999), p. 37.

suitable compensation had been negotiated, Tiffany & Co. created the Tiffany Gold Medal Award for Excellence in American Design, which Hoving presented to Henry Ford II on April 13, 1964, four days before the Mustang went on sale. Aside from the prestige of the Tiffany's name, the award put the Mustang onto the women's pages of a hundred major newspapers, helping to attract the attention of female buyers.

Earlier the same day, Lee Iacocca met with more than 120 representatives from the major newspapers and magazines on the grounds of the 1964 New York World's Fair. Waiting for them was a fleet of seventy-five brand-new Mustangs, which the assembled journalists were invited to drive to Ford's World Headquarters in Dearborn. It was an unprecedented media drive of 750 miles over public roads, and very few of those reporters arrived in Michigan without big grins on their faces.[96] Ford's public-relations office, headed by Walter T. Murphy, also sent out some 11,000 press kits on the Mustang to editors and journalists around the world. In the Mustang's first week on sale, feature articles on the new car appeared in many popular magazines, from *LIFE* to *Esquire*. But Ford's biggest coup was getting the Mustang—and Lee Iacocca—on the covers of both *Time* and *Newsweek* in the same week.[97]

In addition, we purchased full-page ads in 2,600 newspapers and two-dozen major magazines to run the day the car went on sale. John Bowers, the advertising manager, and I also prepared a massive direct-mail campaign aimed at prospective Mustang buyers, mirroring the strategy I had used at Lincoln.

I worked extensively with J. Walter Thompson on the initial Mustang ad campaign. The agency chiefs never forgot how I had gone to bat for them when I was car marketing manager, and they paid me back with some of the best creative work ever. The copy for the early Mustang print

---

96 The automotive press had already been invited to drive the new car on Ford's test track a few weeks earlier so that they could have their stories ready in time for its launch.

97 "Autos: Ford's Young One," *Time*, Vol. 83, No. 16 (April 17, 1964), p. 102, and James C. Jones, "The Mustang—A New Breed Out of Detroit," *Newsweek* (April 20, 1964), p. 100.

ads, generally credited to JWT ad writer Sid Olson,[98] emphasized the Mustang's low price, generous standard equipment, and the ability to customize the car with an array of options.[99] These were all key aspects of the product concept. At my insistence, most of the artwork featured the Mustang in side view,[100] rather than the more customary front or front three-quarter views seen in other automotive ads of the time. JWT had originally proposed using a front view, but I argued strenuously for a profile shot that would show off the Mustang's sleek proportions. Its long hood and short deck would soon come to define the new pony car segment.

My crowning marketing achievement came on the evening of Thursday, April 16: for one half hour during prime time, from nine thirty to ten, every commercial spot on every major television network was filled by an ad for the Ford Mustang. That had never been done before and, as far as I know, has never been done since. Our advertising agency, J. Walter Thompson, wasn't sure they could pull it off when I first suggested the idea. But they did. They bought up as many of the advertising slots as they could and then horse-traded with the other advertisers to free up the rest. We had to give up a lot of prime TV real estate on other days to do it, but it was worth it to make sure that anyone tuning in to one of the three big shows on television that night—*Hazel*, *The Jimmy Dean Show*, or *Perry Mason*—was sure to see the Mustang. We covered the country that night, reaching an unprecedented 29 million households. Later, the Mustang also appeared as part of the story line on *Hazel*, which was sponsored by Ford.

---

98 Olson, a former political speech writer, had coined the phrase "arsenal of democracy" for President Franklin Delano Roosevelt two decades earlier. See Fria, p. 36.

99 The Mustang came standard with various features that normally cost extra on inexpensive cars in those days, such as full carpeting and bucket seats, and buyers could also select fifty factory options, from a vinyl roof to a 289 cu. in. (4,728 cc) V-8 engine. Lee Iacocca says the average Mustang buyer selected almost $1,000 worth of extras, which was hugely profitable for both individual dealers and Ford. See Jones, pp. 97 and 99, and Iacocca, p. 79.

100 E.g., "New Ford Mustang $2,368," advertisement [c. April 1964], reprinted in Terry Ehrich and Richard A. Lentinello, eds., *The Hemmings Book of Mustangs* (Bennington, Vermont: Hemmings Motor News, 2000), p. 13.

◥◆◤

While TV viewers were watching Mustang commercials, the new cars were quietly being unloaded at Ford dealerships across the country. Because so much of the marketing push for the Mustang focused on the car's low price—the basic six-cylinder, stick-shift hardtop started at only $2,368—Lee and I insisted that each dealer have at least one minimally optioned hardtop that would be as close as possible to that advertised price. I had a hell of a time making that happen. I can't remember how many meetings we had with the distribution people. But we managed it.[101]

The Mustang went on sale the morning of Friday, April 17, 1964. With all the publicity, people turned out in droves to see the new car. Over the first weekend alone, Ford dealers were besieged by an estimated 4 million curious and eager customers. Almost 23,000 of them placed orders for the car.[102] Not everyone was content to stand in line: author Robert Fria, who was in his early twenties at the time, would later write that he climbed a dealer's chain-link fence to get a look at the new car.[103] Many people also got a chance to see the Mustang on display at local shopping malls, in bank lobbies, at football games, and in fifteen major airports. We even put them in Holiday Inns!

The Mustang quickly established itself as one of the defining automotive icons of its era. Like the two-seat Thunderbird before it, the Mustang caught the imagination of younger buyers—and quite a few older ones.[104] With the Mustang, Ford had finally found a way to marry

---

101 Another of my ideas for the Mustang was to equalize the freight charges, which in those days varied considerably from region to region. For example, buyers in Los Angeles or Seattle could expect to pay thirty-five to fifty dollars more for freight than a buyer in Dallas. See "The Truth About Car Prices," *Kiplinger's Personal Finance*, Vol. 11, No. 1 (January 1957), p. 23. I wanted to average those costs so that Ford could advertise a single nationwide price, including shipping. I was not successful—the prices quoted in Mustang print ads were FOB (freight on board) Detroit, not including shipping—but my idea was ahead of its time. Today, most U.S. new car buyers pay a uniform destination charge, regardless of region.

102 Brinkley, p. 613.

103 Fria, p. 173.

104 Lee Iacocca says that about one-sixth of all Mustang buyers were forty-five or older. See Iacocca, p. 80.

the original Thunderbird's aspirational appeal to true mass-market sales potential. Although the 1955–1957 Thunderbirds were highly desirable, they were relatively expensive two-seat convertibles. That limited their appeal. The Mustang was even sportier but offered four seats, passable cargo space, and a price a young family could afford. In short, the Mustang was a car that the kids who had stood in line to see the Thunderbird in Ford showrooms a decade earlier could actually own, not just dream about.

And it was a runaway hit.

Ford sold 70,000 Mustangs in the first thirty days and a quarter of a million by the end of the year. Twelve months after its launch that number had climbed to nearly 419,000 units. It was a new industry record, breaking the previous high set in 1960 by Ford's compact Falcon. That had been Iacocca's personal goal. But it didn't stop there; Ford sold one million cars in less than two years,[105] netting a profit of $1.1 billion.[106]

As with the Thunderbird, the Mustang caught General Motors off guard. At the time, Chevrolet had nothing like it. GM's closest equivalent was the Corvair Monza, a sporty version of Chevy's air-cooled, rear-engined compact. The Monza had done well a few years earlier, but the popularity of the Mustang was on a whole other level.[107] Chevrolet dealers did not get a real Mustang rival until the debut of the Camaro in September 1966, which was about the time Ford unveiled the restyled, second-generation Mustang.

By the end of the decade, the Mustang had created a whole genre of sporty cars, including the AMC Javelin, Mercury Cougar, Pontiac Firebird, and Plymouth Barracuda. All carefully followed the Mustang's winning formula and are still collectively known as "pony cars."

---

105 The millionth Mustang was built on Feb. 23, 1966, not quite twenty-four months after Job One. See Fria, p. 178.

106 Iacocca, p. 79.

107 The first-year sales of the Mustang topped the Corvair Monza's best year, 1962, by nearly two to one. See table in Michael Lamm, "Martyr," *Special Interest Autos*, No. 22 (May 1974).

Lee Iacocca deserves full credit for the Mustang's success: the Mustang was 100 percent Lee's car. However, although the vision for the new car was Iacocca's, its execution was very much a collaborative effort. Iacocca's friend Hal Sperlich, whose product-planning work I have long admired,[108] later said, "There's very little accomplished by one man sitting at his desk, having brilliant ideas. Good ideas generally come out of an interaction with many people, and it was that way with the Mustang."[109]

Iacocca's masterstroke in the development of the Mustang was establishing the original Fairlane Committee to outline the parameters for the new car. By meeting off-site and outside normal business hours, the members of that committee were able to speak openly and freely, without any hesitation. It freed guys up to think and express themselves without worrying about some other guy in their department.

It was the kind of collaborative approach that I aimed for when I started setting up Ford's Product Planning Office back in 1949. Back then, I was an army of one, fighting to make the voice of the customer heard inside Ford. Now, Product Planning had come into its own as a central and important part of the corporation. The result was the Ford Mustang.

While I was only one of many important players in the success of the Mustang, the car itself was, perhaps, the ultimate validation of everything I had advocated and fought for throughout my time at Ford. Fifteen years earlier, Ford products had been engineered first and marketed second; the needs of the customer, as I found during my fight to save the V-8, were an afterthought at best. By contrast, the Mustang was shaped not by Engineering or even Styling but by an insightful reading of an emerging market. The way the car was developed became a model for future product planners, both at Ford and in other industries.

---

108 Sperlich, who was fired at the insistence of Henry Ford II in 1976, went on to Chrysler, where he developed the very popular T-115 minivans (Dodge Caravan/Plymouth Voyager/ Chrysler Town & Country). Sperlich was president of Chrysler from 1985 until his retirement in 1988. See Fria, p. 35, and Iacocca, p. 128–130.

109 Quoted in Fria, p. 35.

If the car itself was the culmination of everything I had tried to do in Product Planning, the way we marketed it and sold it amalgamated all the knowledge I had accumulated in sales and marketing, both at Ford and prior to coming to the company, while at the same time breaking a great deal of new ground. Whether print, television, or direct mail, the early Mustang ads made a definite impact. Harold K. Sperlich, who was special-projects assistant to Don Frey during the Mustang's development, later called the Mustang's advertising campaign "the most successful run by any car manufacturer."[110]

My work on the Mustang was the crowning achievement of my career in Dearborn. It would also be my final contribution before leaving Ford.

By the time the car went on sale in April 1964, I had left the company. I had spent the past several years working closely with dealers, and I was intrigued by that side of the business and ready for a new challenge. When the opportunity arose to open my own Ford store in Scottsdale, Arizona, I jumped at it. At a certain point, capital gains become more important than a paycheck. I left Ford on good terms. The company even guaranteed the lease on my property in the desert.

Chase Morsey's Paradise Ford opened for business just as the Mustang arrived in showrooms. I sold cars for four years. Although I enjoyed the business and the opportunity it gave me to participate in a number of civic organizations, I soon found myself longing for a bigger challenge. I had been approached by headhunters through the years. One even asked me if I would be interested in becoming president of American Airlines, though nothing ever came of that. But when Robert Sarnoff offered me a job as vice president of marketing for RCA in 1968, I took it. Not long after that, I decided to get into the oil business.

But no matter what I did, I kept driving Fords—at least until 1977 when I moved to California to marry my second wife, Beverly. She loved her Mercedes as much as I loved my Ford. You can guess who won that argument.

---

110 Quoted in Fria, p. 172.

Conclusion

It has been almost fifty years since I left the Ford Motor Company, but the lessons I learned there and the points I proved are as relevant today as they were half a century ago. In fact, many of them have become axiomatic in today's resurgent American automobile industry.

There is no substitute for understanding the customer. Companies that fail to listen to the men and women who buy their products are headed for disaster. My fight to save the V-8 was motivated by my understanding of this most important tenet of business, and the success Ford enjoyed as a result of listening to my arguments proved their merit.

Unfortunately, Ford and the other American automakers would later forget this. Drunk on their own success, by the end of the 1960s, they would come to take their customers for granted. They convinced themselves that Americans would buy whatever they built, ignored changing customer preferences, and allowed foreign rivals to dominate the industry they had created. The results were disastrous for Detroit and for the nation as a whole.

Fortunately for both, Ford found its way back—and it did it by following the same principles that I lobbied so hard for fifty years earlier. The man responsible for Ford's recent turnaround, Alan Mulally, said the key to the company's revival was to build cars and trucks that people wanted and valued. And he did it, too. Hired by Bill Ford Jr.—the son of William Clay Ford—in September 2006, Mulally soon had the company's factories turning out vehicles that were as good or better than those produced by Toyota and Honda. The critics raved about the new Fords, and influential publications, such as *Consumer Reports*, gave them the highest marks. The American people soon took notice—especially after Mulally turned down a federal bailout in 2009 and told Congress that Ford preferred to fix its problems itself. Ford's sales soared, and it has been the strongest of the Detroit Three ever since, turning in record profits.

Many were surprised by Ford's epic turnaround, but I was not. I found during my time in Dearborn that good products yield good profits. Consumers are not stupid. They want quality and features, and they are willing to pay for them. Too often, companies think otherwise and allow their products to become commodities. In doing so, they cheapen their brand and shrink their own margins. Other companies understand that consumers are willing to pay a premium for products that offer them more of what they need and want. One needs to look no further than the success Apple has enjoyed in recent years to see the truth of this principle. Apple's products cost more than those offered by its rivals, but they also offer more.

Ford, too, has begun charging more for its cars and trucks, because it has invested enough in new technology and manufacturing quality to merit a premium. Under Alan Mulally's leadership, the automaker also has begun making more premium features available as options to its customers. That, too, has helped boost Ford's profits—just as it did when I convinced the company's senior executives to do the same thing back in the 1950s.

I understood the primacy of product because I understood the importance of seeing the big picture. I was able to consider the situations that confronted me at Ford from all angles. I not only understood the point of view of the customers and our dealers but also those of Finance, Engineering, Manufacturing, and Sales. That allowed me to address their concerns even as I strove to make the points that I knew were right.

When Alan Mulally took over as chief executive officer at Ford, he told the other executives, "The data sets you free." That is something I always believed. I used that very principle to convince my superiors at Ford to keep building the V-8. It also proved a powerful weapon in my later battles at the company. It was a lesson I tried to drill into all the men I hired in Product Planning. I would tell them, "It's fine to become passionate about your ideas, but when given the opportunity, you must marshal the facts in such a way that top executives will listen."

That points to another important lesson I learned during my time at Ford: the need to speak up for what you know is right. Simply having an opinion about product decisions, however well-founded, is meaningless if no one in a position of authority ever hears it. That can be a real challenge in organizations that are too bureaucratic. When I read Bob Lutz's description of life inside General Motors, I had to shake my head. How good ideas could ever emerge from beneath so many layers of bureaucracy is beyond me.

When I was asked to head up the new product planning function at Ford, I found myself with a unique and unprecedented opportunity to help shape the future of the company. Then, as now, Ford's future depended on building products that people wanted to buy, and I resolved to be the voice of the customer within the company. Until I stood before Henry Ford II, Ernest Breech, Lewis Crusoe, and the rest of Ford's top brass and made my impassioned plea to save the V-8, that voice had never been heard inside the company's boardroom.

I have no idea how I ever stood up to Crusoe and Breech and the other Ford bigwigs like that. To this day, I still think back on that presentation I made to Henry Ford II and Breech as the toughest meeting of my entire life. In hindsight, it was probably the most reckless move I ever made in my professional career. But it was also the right one—both for me and for the company. Jack Reith later told me that it was only my passion for the V-8 that swayed Crusoe and convinced him to take the matter to Breech. Jack said that after I left the room, Crusoe told him, "The passion he has for the V-8 and the way he explained it cannot be ignored."

I can't imagine how I ever had the nerve to do that. My career at Ford might easily have ended before it had even started. But I didn't think about that then. I just kept thinking about how disappointed Ford customers were going to be about the demise of their beloved V-8. When I think about it now, I understand how brash I must have seemed. The men I confronted were titans of the automobile industry. They had spent their whole adult lives designing, building, and selling cars. They had just invested a huge amount of time trying to come up with a product plan that would turn the company's fortunes around and put the company back on the road to profitability, and then some kid, who hadn't even been on the payroll for two months, came along and told them that they were wrong and that they didn't know what the hell they were doing! Anyone would be a little taken back by that. Like I said, more than sixty years later, I'm still trying to figure out where I came up with the nerve to do it! I guess I was just too young to know any better. But I've always been able to see things. It's a God-given gift, I guess.

Still, it's almost unimaginable that I got those men to change their minds. That they did is a testament to their own considerable skill as leaders. That is particularly true of Breech and Crusoe. Many corporate managers are reluctant to even hear criticism, much less admit they might be wrong. But Breech and Crusoe did—despite the substantial risk to their own reputations—for the simple reason that they realized I was right. That's the sign of a good executive, in my opinion. It reflects a sort of courage that is all too rare in business today.

I was forced to fight hard for many of my proposals, perhaps too hard at times, which I know upset some people. Even though we often disagreed, I had the utmost respect for the many talented stylists, engineers, and executives I worked with at Ford.

The fight over the fate of the V-8 is a missing chapter in the history of the Ford Motor Company. Historians have either overlooked or misunderstood what happened sixty-four years ago in that boardroom in Dearborn. It is hoped that this book will set the matter straight for the first time.

A few years ago, I was reading a *Wall Street Journal* interview with Bert Boeckmann, the owner of the largest Ford dealership in the world, Galpin Ford. Responding to news that Ford was cutting back on production of V-8s and pushing its new V-6 motors instead, he observed that "he learned to be careful years ago not to push a 'V-8 guy' into a six-cylinder car. He kept telling you about the power he was missing."

Reading that gave me pause, because it made me realize just how close the company had come to disaster before I convinced the Product Planning Committee to change its mind and keep building the V-8.

And Boeckmann is not the only one who thinks that people underestimate the continuing draw of the V-8.

"Residents of Manhattan or Beverly Hills may not drive many of what the industry still calls 'full-size pickups.' But in the rest of America, large pickups, such as the (Ford) F-150…are huge sellers. They are mainstream rides in rural America and anywhere you go in Texas," wrote the *Journal*'s own automotive columnist Joe White in 2010. "Most of these trucks roar off dealer lots with big V-8 engines."

Reading such statements today convinces me that the decision to kill the V-8 could well have been a catastrophe for the Ford Motor Company—and that makes me prouder than ever of my decision to stake my career on averting it. Thinking about it now, I think I very well may have saved Ford in the process.

Author's Note

In writing this book, I have done my best to accurately portray these important episodes in the history of the Ford Motor Company. I have relied not only on my own memory of these events but also on the canon of books and articles already published. My aim has been to set the record straight wherever I can. Other authors writing about this period of Ford's history have given me credit for things I did not do and failed to note my contributions in other areas. Unfortunately, many of the original records from this era have not survived in Ford's archives, and many of the people I worked with in those days are now deceased. Those who are still around may recall certain events differently than I do. If I've made any mistakes in this book, they were not intentional.

The main impetus for writing this book came from reading *American Icon: Alan Mulally and the Fight to Save the Ford Motor Company*, a 2012 book by Bryce G. Hoffman, an award-winning journalist who writes about the auto industry for the *Detroit News*. His well-written book is not just a dry history of recent changes at Ford but also an exciting and compelling story. I have spoken at length with Mr. Hoffman, and he has given me many valuable ideas and insights. It is hoped my book's account of events at Ford some sixty-four years ago can come close to the standard he set.

Throughout the writing of this book, I have received a great deal of excellent advice from my good friend, scientist, author, and philanthropist Simon Ramo, known as "Si" to his friends. I consider Si America's foremost man of science. In the 1950s, he helped to develop the first intercontinental ballistic missiles for the U.S. Air Force—the same rockets that later carried the first astronauts into space and helped win the Cold War with the Soviet Union. He was awarded the National Medal of Science by President Carter and the Presidential Medal of Freedom, the country's highest civilian award, by President Reagan. James Woolsey, former director of the CIA, calls Dr. Ramo "the dean of American aerospace technology." I have known Si for over thirty-six years and have been honored to be his friend. It is difficult for me to fully express how grateful I am for our monthly luncheons at the Los Angeles Country Club, especially since he is now one hundred years young and is still as sharp as ever.

My principal researcher and fact-checker for this book was Aaron Severson, who writes about classic cars for *Autoweek* magazine and his own website, *Ate Up With Motor*, winner of the 2012 E.P. Ingersoll Award from the Society of Automotive Historians for the best presentation of automotive history in other than print media. Aaron knows a lot about automotive history and has written many detailed, thoroughly researched articles about cars from around the world. I could not have picked a better person to work with. Aaron has helped me verify my recollections of things that happened more than sixty years ago. He assembled the bibliography and footnotes for the book. He has worked with my drafts and added insights and historical context, suggesting new dimensions for my story and pointing out details I hadn't know before. He has been invaluable to me, and I have especially appreciated his personal interest in completing this book. My thanks to Len Freebern, a Ford fan from Arizona, for introducing me to Aaron.

John Smith, president of the Classic Thunderbird Club International, has been a real help with the Thunderbird chapter of this book. John originally came to see me three or four years ago to talk about the Thunderbird, but our discussions moved on to other areas of my Ford career, particularly my time as Ford's first product planning manager. We agreed that very little had been written about product planning and its importance. John, who is a very good writer, has written several drafts of an article about product planning, but his day job as a bank examiner for the state of Missouri has kept him very busy. I hope he is able to finish his article—I look forward to reading it.

I want to thank Lee Iacocca for giving me the opportunity to work with him on the Mustang. I had many great bosses, but he ranks in the top list.

Finally, a few words about myself, I am now ninety-three years old, living in the Beverly Hills area with my wonderful and talented wife, Beverly, a great artist and the original store designer for Neiman-Marcus in Dallas.

I am still busy running the Morsey Oil & Gas Corporation with the help of our daughter Carol. In addition to that and spending time with our six children and nine grandchildren, I have two main hobbies: model trains and golf.

Though I'm not as good as I used to be, I still play and have been lucky enough to have counted as my partners and friends Arnold Palmer, Gary Player, Ben Hogan, Claude Harmon, Byron Nelson, Sam Snead, Ken Venturi, and Dave Marr. Bing Crosby, a personal friend, was kind enough to invite me to play in his pro-am at Pebble Beach for many years. I was even mentioned once in an article in *Sports Illustrated* about a tournament at Seminole.

After moving to southern California, I joined the Los Angeles Country Club. There, I had the honor of becoming friends with President Ronald Reagan. He and I were golfing buddies and continued to play together long after his mind yielded to dementia. After he passed away in 2004, Nancy Reagan told me how much those outings meant to both of them. Richard Riordan, the former mayor of Los Angeles, once told some dinner guests, "Chase Morsey kept Reagan alive for an extra ten years." If I added a minute to his life, it was the least I could do.

For the last twelve years, I have been building—with a lot of help—a model train layout that covers four rooms in our house and attic. It runs on five levels, and the track is longer than three football fields. It has been my pleasure to entertain many friends and their children with these trains. I even produced a DVD that shows all the action.

Thank you very much for reading my story. I hope you enjoyed it.

Chase Morsey Jr.
Los Angeles, California
July 7, 2013

Bibliography

Books

Adler, Dennis. *Fifties Flashback: The American Car*. Osceola, WI: Motorbooks International, 1996.

Allen, Jim. *Jeep (Collector's Library)*. St. Paul, MN: Motorbooks International, 2004.

Armi, C. Edson. *The Art of American Car Design: The Profession and Personalities*. University Park, PA: Pennsylvania State University Press, 1988.

Askew, Ken. "Motor City Iconoclasts." In *Golden Snapshots: Real Stories by Real People*, edited by D'Angelo and Greene Askew, 21–26. Bloomington, IN: AuthorHouse, 2008.

Auto editors of Consumer Guide. *The Encyclopedia of American Cars: Over 65 Years of Automotive History*. Lincolnwood, IL: Publications International, 1996.

Bonsall, Thomas R. *Disaster in Dearborn: The Story of the Edsel (Automotive History and Personalities)*. Stanford, CA: Stanford General Books, 2002.

——. *The Lincoln Story: The Postwar Years*. Stanford, CA: Stanford General Books, 2004.

Brinkley, Douglas. *Wheels for the World: Henry Ford, His Company, and a Century of Progress*. New York: Viking Penguin, 2003.

Boyer, William P. *Thunderbird: An Odyssey in Automotive Design*. Dallas: Taylor Publishing Company, 1987.

Brock, Ray, and the editors of *Hot Rod* Magazine. "Ford Success Stories: Karol Miller...Bonneville Legend." *Ford Performance Handbook*. Los Angeles: Petersen Publishing: 1962.

Brown, Arch, Richard Langworth, and the auto editors of Consumer Guide. "1949 Ford." In *Great Cars of the 20th Century*, 186–189. Lincolnwood, IL: Publications International, Ltd., 1998.

Byrne, John A. *The Whiz Kids: The Founding Fathers of American Business—and the Legacy They Left Us*. New York: Doubleday, 1993.

Card, Gene A. *Pocono Raceway (Images of Sports: Pennsylvania)*. Mount Pleasant, SC: Arcadia Publishing, 2008.

Collier, Peter, and David Horowitz. *The Fords: An American Epic*. New York: Summit Books, 1987.

Corcoran, Tom. *Mustang 64½—68 (Musclecar Color History)*. Osceola, WI: Motorbooks International, 1993.

Cotter, Tom, and Al Pearce. *Holman Moody: The Legendary Race Team*. Osceola, WI: MBI Publishing, Inc., 2002.

Earley, Helen Jones, and James R. Walkinshaw. *Setting the Pace: Oldsmobile's First 100 Years*. Lansing, MI: Oldsmobile Division of General Motors Corporation, 1996.

Edelstein, Robert. *Full Throttle: The Life and Fast Times of NASCAR Legend Curtis Turner*. New York: Overlook Press, 2006.

Edsall, Larry, and Mike Teske. *Ford Racing Century: A Photographic History of Ford Motorsports*. Osceola, WI: MBI Publishing Company, Inc., 2003.

Farrell, Jim and Cheryl. *Ford Design Department: Concepts and Showcars 1932–1961*. Hong Kong: World Print Ltd., 1999.

Flammang, James M., David L. Lewis, and the auto editors of Consumer Guide. *Ford Chronicle: A Pictorial History from 1893*. Lincolnwood, IL: Publications International, 1992.

Ford Motor Company. *Mechanic's Handbook 1949: Ford Passenger Cars: "V-8" and "6."* Dearborn, MI.: 10 June 1948.

Fria, Robert A. *Mustang Genesis: The Creation of the Pony Car*. Jefferson, NC: McFarland & Company, Inc., 2010.

General Marketing Office, Ford Division, Ford Motor Company. *Knowing What to Do When They Drive Up in an Import…*[Sales training manual, c. April 1969.] Reprinted at The Maverick Page. Ed. Mark S. Gustavason. N.d. www.themaverickpage.com/ Introduction/ Import/import.html. 29 Dec. 2012.

Georgano, Nick, and Nicky Wright. *Art of the American Automobile: The Greatest Stylists and Their Work*. New York: Smithmark Publishers, 1995.

Granatelli, Anthony (Andy). *They Call Me Mister 500.* Chicago: Henry Regnery Company/Bantam Books, 1970.

Gunnell, John, ed. *Standard Catalog of American Cars 1946–1975.* Rev 4th ed. Iola, WI: Krause Publications, 2002.

———. *Standard Catalog of Light-Duty Ford Trucks 1905–2002.* Iola, WI: Krause Publications, 2003.

———. *T-Bird: 40 Years of Thunder.* Iola, WI: Krause Publications, 1995.

Halberstam, David. *The Reckoning.* New York: William Morrow and Company, 1986.

Hoffman, Bryce G. *American Icon: Alan Mulally and the Fight to Save Ford Motor Company.* New York: Crown Business, 2012.

Hunter, Don, and Al Pearce. *The Illustrated History of Stock Car Racing.* Osceola, WI: MBI Publishing, 1998.

Iacocca, Lee, with William Novak. *Iacocca: An Autobiography.* New York: Bantam Books, 1984.

Katz, John F. *Soaring Spirit: Thirty Five Years of the Ford Thunderbird.* Kutztown, PA: Automobile Quarterly, Inc., 1989.

Lamm, Michael, and Dave Holls. *Century of Automotive Style: 100 Years of American Car Design.* Stockton, CA: Lamm-Morada Publishing Co. Inc., 1997.

Langworth, Richard M. *The Thunderbird Story: Personal Luxury.* Osceola, WI: Motorbooks International, 1980.

Langworth, Richard M., and the auto editors of Consumer Guide. *The Complete Book of Corvette.* New York: Beekman House, 1987.

Leffingwell, Randy. *Corvette: America's Sports Car.* Osceola, WI: Motorbooks International, 1997.

———. *Mustang: America's Classic Pony Car.* Ann Arbor, MI: Lowe & B. Hould Pub., 1999.

Leffingwell, Randy, and David Newhardt. *Mustang: Forty Years.* St. Paul, MN: Crestline/MBI Publishing/Barnes & Noble Publishing Inc., 2006.

Levine, Leo. *Ford: The Dust and the Glory, a Racing History.* New York: The Macmillan Company, 1968.

Lutz, Robert. *Car Guys vs. Bean Counters: The Battle for the Soul of American Business*. New York: Penguin, 2011.

McCormack, Mark H. *The Terrible Truth About Lawyers: How Lawyers Really Work and How to Deal with Them*. Sag Harbor, NY: Beech Tree Books, 1987.

Mueller, Mike. *Classic Corvette: The First Thirty Years*. Osceola, WI: MBI Publishing Company, 2002.

——. *Motor City Muscle: The High-Powered History of the American Muscle Car*. Osceola, WI: Motorbooks International, 1997.

——. *Pickup Trucks*. Ann Arbor, MI: Lowe & B. Hould Publishers, 2001.

Parris, Michael. *Fords of the Fifties*. Tucson, AZ.: California Bill's Automotive Handbooks, 2000.

Pierce, Daniel S. *Real NASCAR: White Lightning, Red Clay, and Big Bill France*. Chapel Hill, NC: University of North Carolina Press, 2010.

Productioncars.com. *Book of Automobile Production and Sales Figures, 1945–2005*. N.p.: 2006.

Reynolds, Stacey L., and the Flat Rock Historical Society. *Flat Rock (Images of America)*. Charleston, SC: Arcadia Publishing, 2011.

Sifakis, Carl. *The Mafia Encyclopedia*. Second edition. New York: Checkmark Books/Facts on File, Inc., 1999.

Sorenson, Charles E., with Samuel T. Williamson. *My Forty Years with Ford*. New York: W.W. Norton, 1956.

Tanner, Hans. *The Racing Fords*. New York: Meredith Press, 1968.

Temple, David W. *Full-Size Fords: 1955–1970*. Denver: CarTech, Inc., 2010.

Thompson, Neal. *Driving with the Devil: Southern Moonshine, Detroit Wheels, and the Birth of NASCAR*. New York: Crown Publishing Group, 2006.

USAF Historical Division. *The Army Air Forces in World War II Vol. VI: Men and Planes*. Second edition. Eds. W.F. Craven and J.L. Cate. Chicago: The University of Chicago Press, 1955.

Warnock, C. Gayle. *The Rest of the Edsel Affair*. Bloomington, IN: AuthorHouse, 2007.

Wilkins, Mira, and Frank Ernest Hill. *American Business Abroad: Ford on Six Continents*. New York: Cambridge University Press, 2011.

Wright, J. Patrick. *On a Clear Day You Can See General Motors: John Z. DeLorean's Look Inside the Automotive Giant*. Chicago: Avon Books, 1979.

Young, Anthony, and Mike Mueller. *Classic Chevy Hot Ones: 1955–1957*. Second ed. Ann Arbor, MI: Lowe & B. Hould Publishers, 2002.

Chase Morsey Jr., born in St. Louis in 1919, became part of an elite Army Air Force team dedicated to using business management principles to manage the World War II air campaign over Germany and Japan. He left the military to help save struggling Ford Motor Company, where his passion led him to save the V-8 engine and preserve Ford's role in automotive history.

Morsey played a crucial role in the creation of some of Ford's most iconic vehicles, including the Ford Thunderbird and Mustang. He got Ford into NASCAR and convinced famous golfers to market Lincolns.

Morsey went on to become the chief financial officer of RCA after opening up his own Ford dealership in Arizona. He eventually moved to southern California, where he became former president Ronald Reagan's golfing buddy at the Los Angeles Country Club. He continues to reside in Los Angeles with his wife Beverly.

Index

Made in the USA
Charleston, SC
17 March 2016